GCSE Physics
Essential Exam Practice

It's packed with lots of nasty questions — because they're
the sort you'll get in the exam.

They're organised by topic, so you can easily see the types of questions
you might get on each area of the syllabus.

Practise getting these questions right and you'll
sweat a lot less on the big day.

Contents

Section One — Electricity and Magnetism
Current, Voltage and Resistance 1
Circuit Symbols and Devices 2
Series Circuits 3
Parallel Circuits 4
Static Electricity 5
Static Electricity — Examples 6
Energy in Circuits 7
The Cost of Domestic Electricity 8
Mains Electricity 9
The National Grid 10
Magnetic Fields 11
Electromagnets 12
Electromagnetic Devices 13
The Motor Effect 14
Electromagnetic Induction 15
Transformers 16
Electricity and Magnetism Mini-Exam (1) 17
Electricity and Magnetism Mini-Exam (2) 18
Electricity and Magnetism Mini-Exam (3) 19
Electricity and Magnetism Mini-Exam (4) 20

Section Two — Forces and Motion
Gravity, Weight and Moments 21
Force Diagrams and Friction 22
The Three Laws of Motion 23
Speed, Velocity and Acceleration 24
Distance-Time and Velocity-Time Graphs 25
Resultant Force and Terminal Velocity 26
Stopping Distances for Cars 27
Hooke's Law 28
Boyle's Law: $P_1V_1 = P_2V_2$ 29
Forces and Motion Mini-Exam (1) 30
Forces and Motion Mini-Exam (2) 31
Forces and Motion Mini-Exam (3) 32

Section Three — Waves
Waves — Basic Principles 33
Sound Waves 34
Ultrasound 35
Questions on the Speed of Sound 36
Reflection: a Property of all Waves 37
Refraction: a Property of all Waves 38
Refraction: Two Special Cases 39
Uses of Total Internal Reflection 40
Digital and Analogue Signals 41
Diffraction: a Property of all Waves 42
The Electromagnetic Spectrum 43
Microwaves and Infrared 44
Visible and UV Light, X-Rays and Gamma Rays 45
Seismic Waves 46
Earth's Structure 47
Evidence for Plate Tectonics 48
Plate Boundaries 49
Waves Mini-Exam (1) 50
Waves Mini-Exam (2) 51
Waves Mini-Exam (3) 52
Waves Mini-Exam (4) 53

Section Four — Outer Space
The Planets 54
Moons, Meteorites, Asteroids and Comets 55
Satellites 56
Searching for Life on Other Planets 57
The Universe 58
The Life Cycle of Stars 59
The Origin of the Universe 60
The Origin and Future of the Universe 61
Outer Space Mini-Exam (1) 62
Outer Space Mini-Exam (2) 63
Outer Space Mini-Exam (3) 64

Section Five — Energy
Energy Transfer 65
Conservation of Energy & Efficiency of Machines 66
Work Done, Energy and Power 67
Kinetic Energy and Potential Energy 68
Heat Transfer 70
Conduction, Convection, and Radiation of Heat 71
Applications of Heat Transfer
 & Keeping Buildings Warm 72
Energy Resources 73
Power Stations Using Non-Renewables 74
Wind Power and Hydroelectric Power 75
Wave Power and Tidal Power 76
Geothermal and Wood Burning 77
Solar Energy and Comparisons 78
Energy Mini-Exam (1) 79
Energy Mini-Exam (2) 80
Energy Mini-Exam (3) 81
Energy Mini-Exam (4) 82

Section Six — Radioactivity
Atomic Structure and Isotopes 83
The Three Types of Radiation 84
Background Radiation 85
Uses of Radioactive Materials 86
Detection of Radiation 88
Radiation Hazards and Safety 89
Nuclear Equations and Half-Life 90
Half-Life Calculations 91
Radioactivity Mini-Exam (1) 92
Radioactivity Mini-Exam (2) 93
Radioactivity Mini-Exam (3) 94

Published by Coordination Group Publications Ltd.

Contributors:
Tony Alldridge, Peter Cecil, Vikki Cunningham, Andrew Furze, Simon Little, Kate Manson, Barbara Mascetti, Steve Parkinson, Kate Redmond, James Paul Wallis, Andy Williams

ISBN: 1 84146 225 X

Groovy website: www.cgpbooks.co.uk

With thanks to John Mosely for the proofreading.
Jolly bits of clipart from CorelDRAW
Printed by Elanders Hindson, Newcastle upon Tyne

Text, design, layout and original illustrations © Coordination Group Publications Ltd. 2004
All rights reserved.

Section One — Electricity and Magnetism

Current, Voltage and Resistance

1. The diagram shows a circuit used to show that sodium chloride solution conducts electricity.

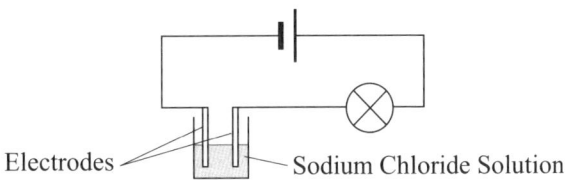

Electrodes — Sodium Chloride Solution

(a) Name and give the charge of the particles responsible for the flow of electric current through the filament of the lamp.

....

(b) What happens to the current in this circuit if the voltage of the power supply is increased?

....

(c) Explain how the current flows through the sodium chloride solution.

....

....

2. The diagram shows the circuit of an electric heater.

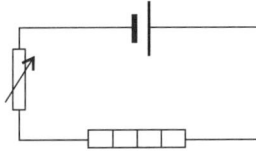

How does the current flowing in this circuit change depending on the variable resistor setting?

....

3. Our mains electricity is alternating current (AC), but a torch battery supplies direct current (DC).

(a) Explain the difference between AC and DC.

....

....

(b) Complete these diagrams showing the CRO traces for AC and DC.

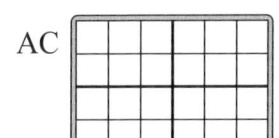

Section One — Electricity and Magnetism

Circuit Symbols and Devices

1. A student collects a set of voltage and current readings for a filament lamp. She uses this circuit but she has left out the meter symbols.

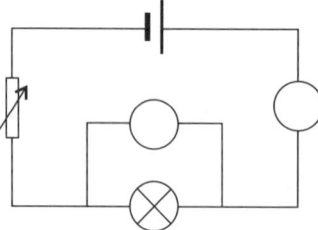

   (a) Add suitable meter symbols to the circuit diagram.

   (b) Sketch the shape of the graph that she would obtain.

   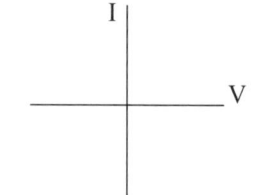

   (c) When the filament lamp is at full brightness it takes 1.6 A of current from the 12 V power supply. Calculate the resistance of the filament lamp.

   ....

2. A thermistor is a component often used in electronic equipment to sense temperature changes.

   (a) (i) Draw the circuit symbol for a thermistor.

   (ii) Complete this graph to show how the resistance of a thermistor changes with temperature.

   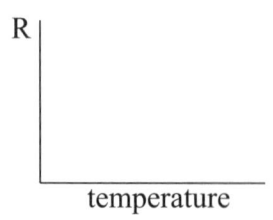

   (b) A thermistor is used in a heating control system. The current flowing through the thermistor is kept constant at 120 mA. Calculate the change in potential difference (p.d.) across the thermistor when its resistance changes from 40 Ω to 50 Ω.

   ....

3. Name the electrical component represented by this circuit symbol, and describe its function.

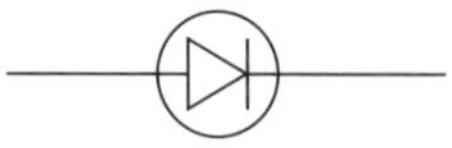

....

....

Section One — Electricity and Magnetism

Series Circuits

1   The diagram shows a series circuit used to control the speed of a toy racing car.

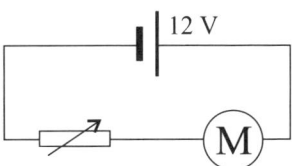

   (a) Why are the variable resistor and the motor connected in series and not in parallel?

   ....

   ....

   (b) Find the voltage across the motor when the voltage across the variable resistor is 5.5 V.

   ....

   (c) As the resistance of the variable resistor is increased, which one of the following is correct?

	Voltage across variable resistor	Voltage across motor	Current flowing
A	decreases	increases	decreases
B	increases	decreases	decreases
C	decreases	increases	increases
D	increases	decreases	increases

   ....

2   The diagram shows a circuit in which three resistors are connected in series.

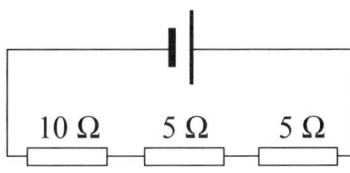

   (a) Calculate the total resistance of the 3 resistors.

   ....

   (b) Given that the p.d. across the 10 Ω resistor is 4 V, find:

      (i) The current flowing in this circuit.

      ....

      (ii) The power supply voltage.

      ....

Section One — Electricity and Magnetism

Parallel Circuits

1. This question is about parallel circuits.

   (a) Give two reasons why the lights in a house are connected in parallel rather than in series.

   ....

   ....

   (b) The diagram shows a parallel circuit with ammeters used to measure the current at three points in the circuit. What rule links the readings on A_1, A_2 and A_3?

   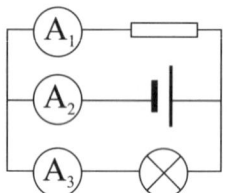

   ....

2. The diagram shows a circuit similar to that used for the lights on a car.
   Each headlight bulb is rated at 12 V 6 A and each side light bulb is rated at 12 V 0.5 A.

   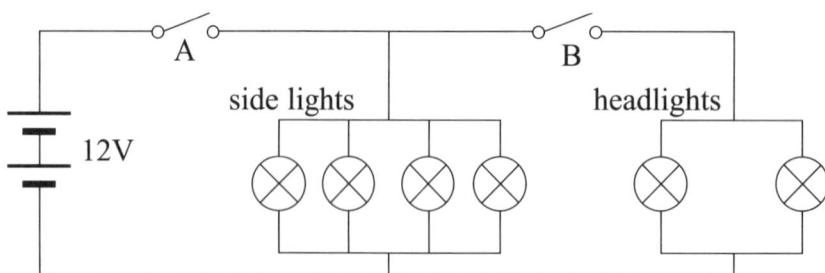

   (a) Calculate the total current flowing from the battery when:

   (i) Switch A is closed and switch B is open.

   ....

   (ii) Switch A is open and switch B is closed.

   ....

   (iii) Switches A and B are both closed.

   ....

   (b) The connections to the car's heated rear window are not shown in the diagram.
   Explain why the car's lights dim slightly when the rear window heater is switched on.

   ....

   ....

Static Electricity

1. When an acetate rod is rubbed with a cloth the rod becomes positively charged. The rod will then attract small uncharged pieces of tissue paper.

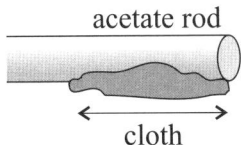
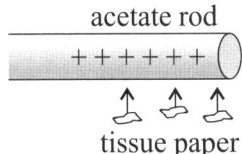

(a) Which of the following happens as the acetate rod becomes charged? Tick the correct answer.

☐ Protons move from rod to cloth.   ☐ Protons move from cloth to rod.

☐ Electrons move from rod to cloth.   ☐ Electrons move from cloth to rod.

(b) Explain why the rod attracts an uncharged piece of tissue paper.

....

....

....

....

(c) Some railways use overhead electric cables at a voltage of 25 kV (25 000 V).

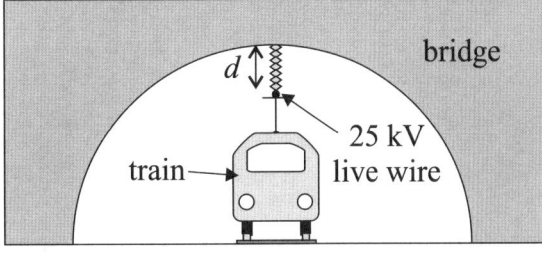

(i) Suggest why the cables have to be kept a certain distance d away from bridges and other structures.

....

....

(ii) How would d need to be changed if the railway company decided to increase the supply voltage?

....

Section One — Electricity and Magnetism

Static Electricity — Examples

1. The diagram shows part of an ink-jet printer. Each droplet of ink is given a positive charge as it leaves the nozzle. Plates A and B are also charged.

   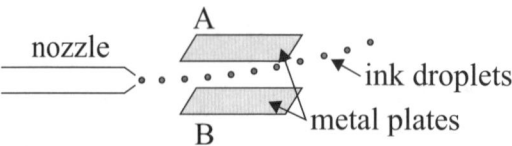

   (a) What charges would plates A and B have to make the droplets bend upwards as shown?

   ....

   (b) Explain how the droplets can be steered up or down to any desired position.

   ....

   ....

   (c) Give one reason why it is important that the droplets produced are all the same size.

   ....

2. The diagram shows a family car at the end of a journey. The car body has a positive electric charge.

   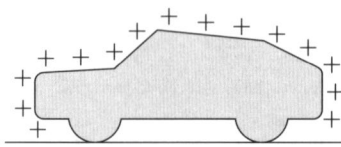

   (a) When the driver gets out and touches the car she gets a small electric shock. Explain why.

   ....

   ....

   (b) The diagram shows an aircraft being refuelled. No safety precautions have been taken.

   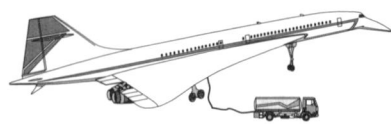

   (i) Explain how static electricity could cause an explosion in this situation.

   ....

   ....

   (ii) Give one precaution that can be taken to avoid this danger.

   ....

Section One — Electricity and Magnetism

Energy in Circuits

1. Complete the following tables showing the energy transfers associated with components in electric circuits. The first one has been done for you.

component	energy transfer
resistor	electrical → thermal
LED	

component	energy transfer
cell	
motor	

2. Two simple electric immersion heaters are made using different resistance wires of identical length and thickness. The heaters are placed in identical beakers containing equal volumes of water and connected to the same power supply voltage. The temperature of water in each beaker is recorded over a period of time.

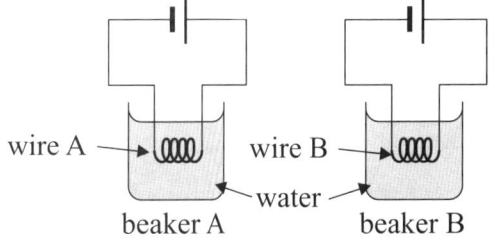

The water temperature in beaker A rises faster than in beaker B. What does this tell you about the two wires? Explain your answer.

....

....

3. A motor is connected to a 3 V battery as shown in the diagram.

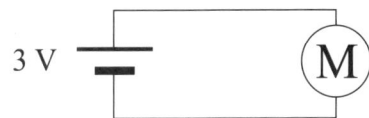

(a) Calculate the energy transferred to the motor when 10 C of electrical charge passes through it.

....

(b) A series resistor is now added to the circuit.

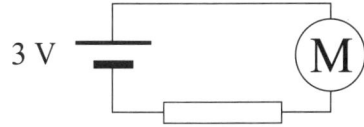

When 10 C of charge pass around this circuit, 8 J of energy are dissipated in the resistor.

(i) Find the p.d. across the resistor.

....

(ii) Find the energy transferred to the motor by the 10 C of charge.

....

Section One — Electricity and Magnetism

The Cost of Domestic Electricity

1. Which of the following equations is correct?

    A   Energy in joules = (Power in watts) × (Time in seconds)

    B   Energy in joules = (Power in watts) ÷ (Time in seconds)

    C   Energy in watts = (Power in joules) × (Time in seconds)

    D   Energy in watts = (Power in joules) ÷ (Time in seconds)

2. Sally's electricity bill states that she has used 500 units in the last quarter (the last 3 months).

    (a) What is meant by a "unit" of electricity?

    ....

    (b) Convert 500 units to megajoules (MJ).

    ....

    (c) The electricity company charges 8 p per unit.
    Find the cost of leaving a 100 W security lamp switched on for 6 hours.

    ....

    (d) Calculate Sally's bill if there is a fixed quarterly charge of £8.50.

    ....

3. Sam lives in a rented flat. He has to put coins in his electricity meter to use the 3 kW electric fire.

    50 p   50 p   50 p

    Sam finds that one 50 p coin will run the fire for 90 minutes.

    (a) How many units does Sam get for his 50 p?

    ....

    (b) Sam's landlord collects the coins and pays the electricity company 10 p per unit.
    How much profit does Sam's landlord make on each unit used?

    ....

Section One — Electricity and Magnetism

Mains Electricity

1   The diagram shows a standard mains plug.

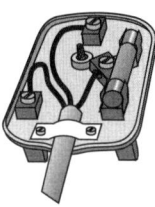

(a) Complete the passage below by filling in the missing words.

The three wires connected in a 3-pin plug are called .... (coloured brown), ... (coloured blue) and earth (coloured ....). To protect the appliance when it is plugged in there is a fuse which is connected to the .... wire. The earth wire is connected to all appliances that have .... cases.

This is to prevent the person using it getting an electric shock.

(b) What is the average value of the mains voltage? Underline the correct answer.

    12 V   230 A   40 000 V   230 V

2   Electrical appliances are carefully designed to prevent you getting an electric shock.

(a) A washing machine develops a fault. Part of the live wire touches the metal case. Explain how the earth wire and fuse work together to prevent you getting an electric shock.

....

....

(b) Bob buys a new television set. When he looks at the instruction booklet he notices that there are only two wires in the plug. The booklet tells him that the TV is "double insulated".

   (i) Which two wires are in the plug?

....

   (ii) Why do we say the TV is "double insulated"?

....

....

Section One — Electricity and Magnetism

The National Grid

1. (a) What current flows in a television rated at 300 W that is plugged into a 230 V mains supply?

   ....

   (b) What is the correct size of fuse to put into the plug attached to the television?
   Fuses available are: 1 A, 3 A, 5 A, 13 A

   ....

   (c) Explain your choice in part (b).

   ....

2. Look at the diagram of part of the National Grid:

   1 000 000 W (1 megawatt) from power station → 1 → 2 → to factory

   (a) What name is given to the devices at 1 and 2?

   ....

   (b) Explain how the functions of device 1 and device 2 differ.

   ....

   (c) Which part of the National Grid would not be able to work with DC electricity?

   ....

   (d) If the voltage was 25 000 V in the pylon cables, what would the current be?

   ....

   (e) What would the current be if the voltage were increased to 400 000 V?

   ....

   (f) The amount of heat lost from the cables depends on the current.
   Use your answers to (d) and (e) to explain why power stations transmit at very high voltage.

   ....

   ....

Section One — Electricity and Magnetism

Magnetic Fields

1. The diagram below shows plotting compasses being used to show magnetic field lines. One of the compass needles is drawn on.

   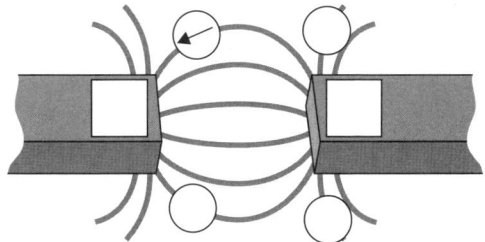

   (a) Put arrows on the other three compasses to show which way they would point.

   (b) Label the poles of the two magnets by putting a letter in each of the square boxes.

   (c) Complete this definition:

   A magnetic .... is a region where a magnetic material,

   such as .... or .... experiences a

   ....

   (d) Give one similarity between a bar magnet and a solenoid.

   ....

   ....

   (e) On the diagram below, draw the shape of the magnetic field around the wire and show its direction.

   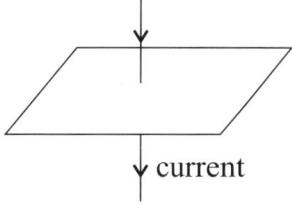

2. Gary decides to use a bar magnet as a compass.
   He hangs it from a thread and holds it up.

   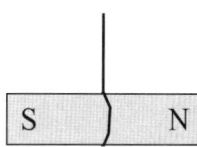

   It stops swinging. The magnet hangs so that its south pole points the same way as Gary is facing. What direction is Gary facing? Explain your answer.

   ....

   ....

Section One — Electricity and Magnetism

Electromagnets

1. Look at the two solenoids below. They are both wound onto a soft iron core, and the same current is applied to each. The core is the same size for both solenoids.

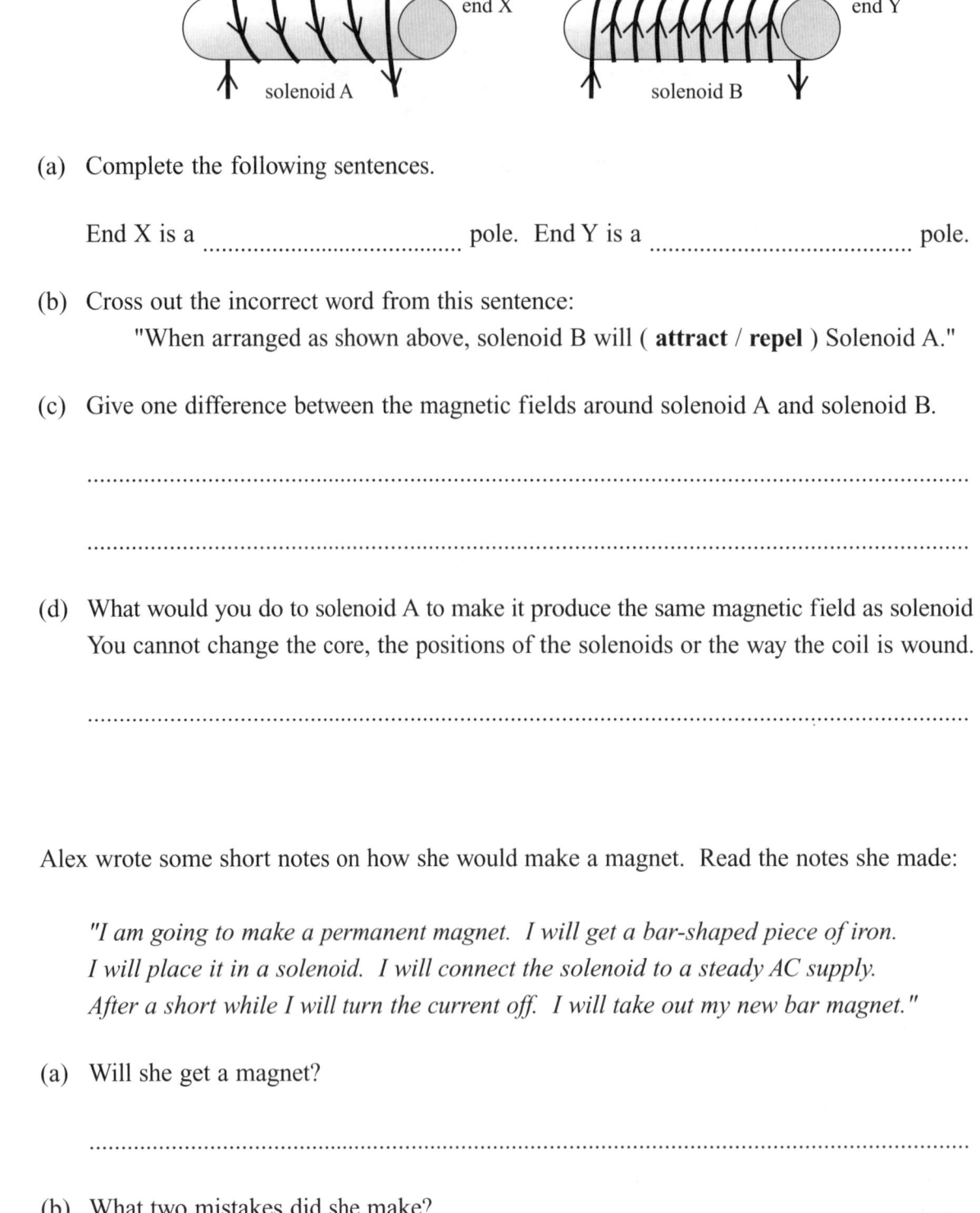

(a) Complete the following sentences.

End X is a .... pole. End Y is a .... pole.

(b) Cross out the incorrect word from this sentence:
   "When arranged as shown above, solenoid B will (**attract** / **repel**) Solenoid A."

(c) Give one difference between the magnetic fields around solenoid A and solenoid B.

   ....

   ....

(d) What would you do to solenoid A to make it produce the same magnetic field as solenoid B? You cannot change the core, the positions of the solenoids or the way the coil is wound.

   ....

2. Alex wrote some short notes on how she would make a magnet. Read the notes she made:

   "I am going to make a permanent magnet. I will get a bar-shaped piece of iron. I will place it in a solenoid. I will connect the solenoid to a steady AC supply. After a short while I will turn the current off. I will take out my new bar magnet."

   (a) Will she get a magnet?

   ....

   (b) What two mistakes did she make?

   ....

   ....

Section One — Electricity and Magnetism

Electromagnetic Devices

1. When a current is applied to an electromagnet, a magnetic field is produced.

   (a) Complete the following description by crossing out the wrong word.

   An electromagnet is made by winding a lot of turns of wire on a (**hard** / **soft**) (**iron** / **steel**) core. The core (**increases** / **decreases**) the strength of the electromagnet.

   (b) Which of the following will be separated from a pile of metal using an electromagnet? Underline the correct answer(s).

   silver coin   steel nail   brass ornament   aluminium can   nickel-plated spoon

2. Look at the incomplete diagram of an electric bell that uses electromagnets.

   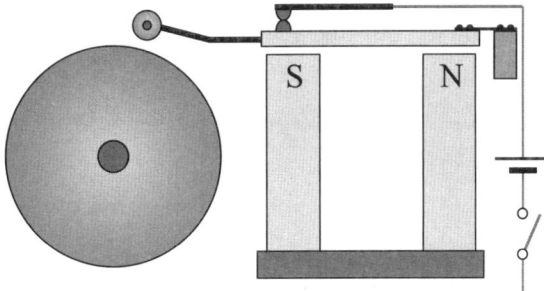

   Complete the diagram by drawing in the wire. Make sure you connect it to the battery.
   NB: the electromagnets need to be wound to make sure the magnetic poles are the ones shown on the diagram — use arrows to show which way the coils are wound.

3. Circuit breakers are often used in place of fuses.

   (a) Where in the circuit is the circuit breaker positioned?

   ....

   (b) "A circuit breaker can also be called a resettable fuse."
   Explain what this means. Your explanation must use the term "electric current".

   ....

   ....

   ....

Section One — Electricity and Magnetism

The Motor Effect

1 The diagram shows a loudspeaker connected to a cell.

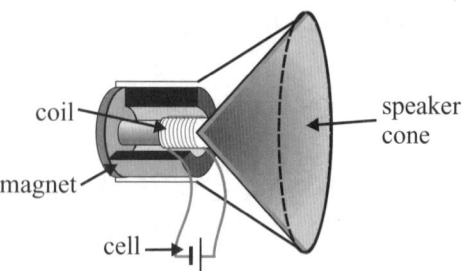

(a) What would happen to the coil at the centre?

....

(b) What would happen to the speaker cone?

....

(c) What would you hear? Explain your answer.

....

....

2 The diagram below shows a simple motor. The coil is rotating as shown.

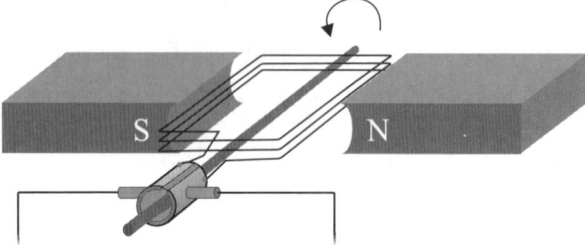

(a) On the diagram, label the split ring commutator, the coil and the permanent magnets.

(b) Use arrows to mark on the diagram the direction of the force on each arm of the coil.

(c) Draw on arrows to show the direction the current is flowing.

(d) Draw a +/– on the commutator leads to show the direction the battery is connected.

(e) Give two ways of increasing the speed of this motor.

....

....

Section One — Electricity and Magnetism

Electromagnetic Induction

1 The diagram shows a model dynamo.

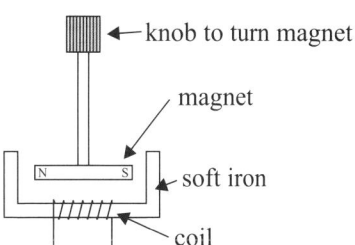

(a) What happens in the coil when the magnet is rotated clockwise? Explain your answer.

....

....

(b) What difference would you notice if the magnet was rotated anticlockwise?

....

The dynamo is attached to a cathode ray oscilloscope (CRO). You turn the dynamo and get the output shown on diagram A:

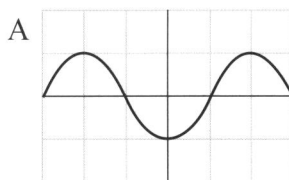 

(c) What type of voltage is this? ....

(d) On Diagram B draw what you would expect to see if you spin the dynamo twice as fast.

2 "The size of the induced voltage is proportional to the rate of change of flux through the circuit."

(a) What do you understand by rate of change of flux?

....

(b) The magnets in diagram D are twice as strong as those in diagram C.

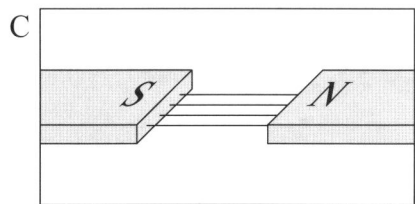 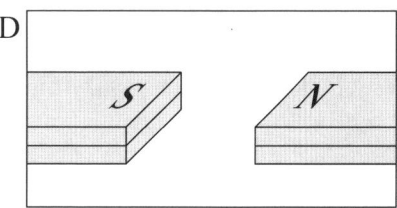

(i) On diagram C draw arrows to show the direction of the field lines.

(ii) Draw on diagram D the lines of magnetic flux.

Section One — Electricity and Magnetism

Transformers

1   The diagram shows a transformer.

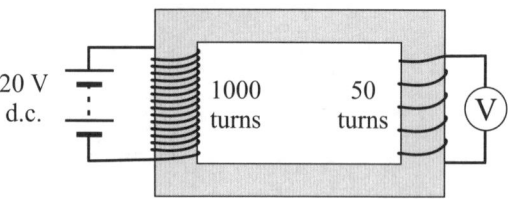

(a) (i) What type of transformer is this?

....

(ii) What is the other type of transformer called?

....

(b) How many turns are there on

(i) the primary coil?

....

(ii) the secondary coil?

....

(c) What is the ratio of the turns on this transformer?

....

(d) Look carefully at the circuit. What is the output voltage? Give a reason for your answer.

....

(e) Transformers are usually wound on a laminated core.

(i) Name the metal used for the core of the transformer.

....

(ii) Why is the core a necessary part of a transformer?

....

(iii) What would happen if the core was not laminated?

....

Section One — Electricity and Magnetism

Electricity and Magnetism Mini-Exam (1)

1 Raana and Emma did an experiment to look at the resistance of different wires.

(a) Raana measured the current using a 1 A ammeter. She measured the potential difference with a 6 V voltmeter. She plotted her results on the graph as shown.

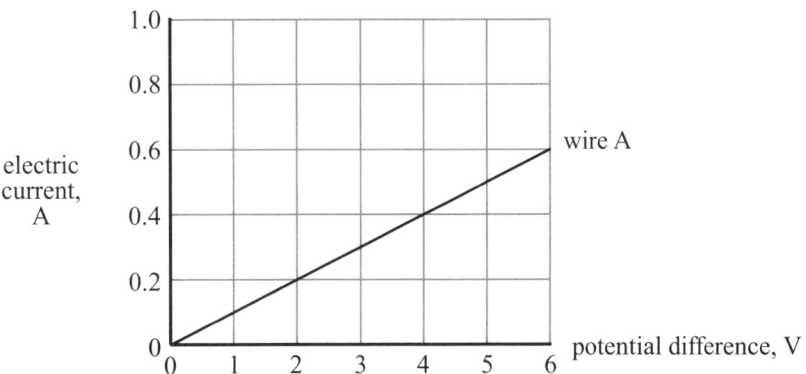

Emma used the same apparatus, this time measuring wire B. Her results are shown below.

potential difference, V	0.0	1.0	2.0	3.0	4.0	5.0
electric current, A	0.0	0.2	0.4	0.6	0.8	1.0

(i) Plot her results on the graph next to Raana's. Label the graph "Wire B".

(ii) Why did Emma not take a current reading at 6 V?

....

(iii) Use the graph to compare the resistance of wires A and wire B.

....

....

(iv) Emma drew her circuit as shown below. She forgot to draw in the meters she used.

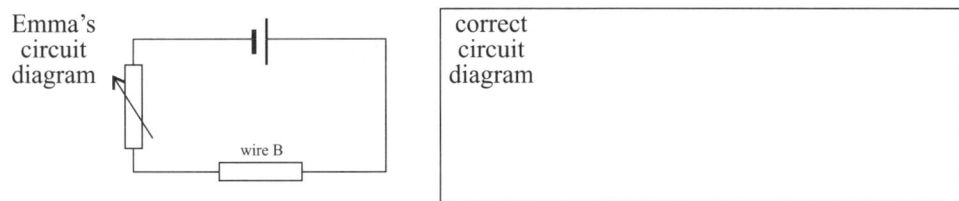

Redraw the circuit diagram, including appropriate meters.

(b) Robin uses the same apparatus to investigate the resistance of a filament lamp. Describe how you would expect his results to differ from the results for a wire.

....

....

Electricity and Magnetism Mini-Exam (2)

2   This question is about static electricity. A duster is rubbed on a polythene rod.
    The rod becomes charged with a negative static charge.

   (a) (i) Explain how the rod becomes charged.

        ....

        ....

       (ii) What happens to the charge on the duster?

        ....

       (iii) An acetate rod is brought next to the polythene rod as shown below.
             They move closer together.

             What charge is on the acetate rod?

        ....

   (b) Ann is wearing slippers with plastic soles.
       She walks on a carpet made from a synthetic material.
       She touches the metal radiator and gets a small shock. Explain why Ann felt a shock.

        ....

        ....

3   This question is about generating electricity.

   (a) In a gas-fired power station, energy is transferred from gas to electricity.

       furnace and boiler   turbine   generator   transformer   electricity to grid

       (i) Use the diagram to explain how the electricity is generated.

        ....

        ....

        ....

Section One — Electricity and Magnetism

Electricity and Magnetism Mini-Exam (3)

(ii) The transformer steps-up the voltage to a very high level for transmission through the national grid. Explain why.

....

....

(b) Lee wants to light a 12 V bulb from a 2 V AC power supply.
He decides to make a simple transformer. The primary coil has 20 turns.
How many turns should the secondary coil have in order to make the bulb light normally?

....

....

4   Alex builds two circuits using 6 V DC power supplies and identical bulbs.

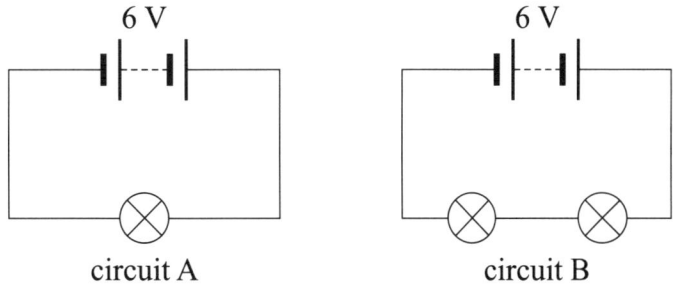

(a) The p.d. (voltage) across the bulb in circuit A is 6 V.
The current through the bulb is 0.25 A.
Calculate the resistance of the bulb.

....

(b) Explain what Alex will see when he builds circuit B.
Use the words current and resistance in your answer.

....

....

(c) Using the same power supply and bulbs, how could Alex make the two bulbs glow brighter?

....

Electricity and Magnetism Mini-Exam (4)

5   This question is about electricity in the home. Look at the diagram below.
    It shows the wiring for a room in Tony's house.

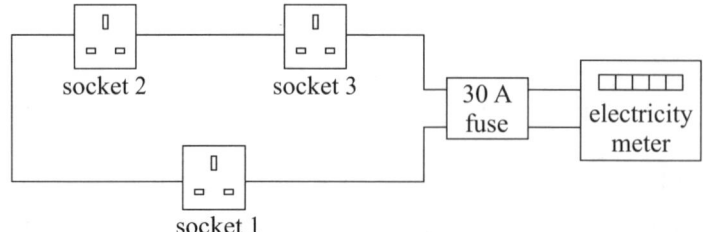

There are three sockets. Each electrical socket can deliver a maximum current of 13 A.

(a)   Tony buys two identical fan heaters. The electrical information is shown on a small information plate on the back of each heater.

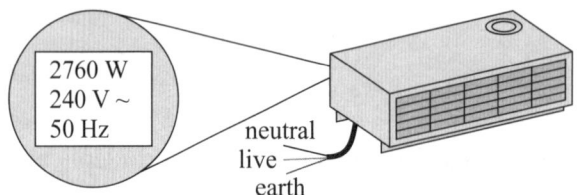

What current does one heater need when it is turned on full power?

....

(b)   He plugs each heater into a socket. He turns them on full power. His room gets warm. He then plugs his kettle into the last socket. The kettle needs a current of 9 A to work. Everything stops working. Explain why.

....

....

(c)   The heater has three wires in the cable.

   (i)   Which wire is connected to the fuse?   ....

   (ii) What is the job of the earth wire?

   ....

   ....

(d)   A hair dryer is rated at 1000 W. Electricity costs 6 p per unit (kilowatt-hour). The hair dryer is used for half an hour each day. How much does it cost to use the hair dryer for one week?

....

Section One — Electricity and Magnetism

Section Two — Forces and Motion

Gravity, Weight and Moments

1. This question is about Geoff (mass 90 kg), who is working on a building site on Earth.
   On Earth, the gravitational field strength is 10 N/kg.

   (a) Explain the difference between Geoff's mass and his weight.

   ....

   ....

   (b) Calculate Geoff's weight.

   ....

   (c) Geoff uses a strong steel bar to try to lift a stone slab.

   ←—— 1.5 m ——→←— 0.5 m —→

   The slab proves to be difficult to lift, and Geoff rests the bar on a smaller stone as a pivot.
   He places the pivot in a position where the moment generated by his weight is exactly
   balanced by the moment generated by the weight of the slab.

   (i) Calculate the moment which Geoff's weight produces about the pivot.

   ....

   (ii) Use this to calculate the force which the slab exerts downwards at the other end of
   the pivot.

   ....

2. A mission is planned to send astronauts to the Moon.
   When they get to the Moon, the astronauts climb down a ladder to the surface.
   They can't use the ladder on the Earth because it is too flimsy.
   Explain why the ladder will be useable on the Moon.

   ....

   ....

Force Diagrams and Friction

1. The diagram below represents the cab of a heavy goods vehicle. It is parked at a service station.

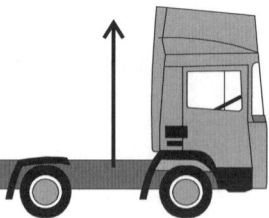

(a) Label the upward force shown on the diagram.

(b) Add an arrow to show the other main force acting on the cab. Label this force.

(c) The old design for the cab, and a new version are shown below.
The two designs contain the same engine.

   (i) What force, experienced by the cab when it is moving, is the new design intended to reduce?

   ....

   (ii) Explain how this reduction has been achieved.

   ....

   (iii) It is found that the new design also has a higher top speed.
   Explain why the change has led to a higher top speed.

   ....

   ....

(d) Many parts of the cab are designed to reduce friction.
For example, grease is used in the bearings to reduce friction between the moving parts.
Suggest a part of the cab where it is desirable to have a **high** friction force.

....

Section Two — Forces and Motion

The Three Laws of Motion

1 The diagram shows Karl jumping off his skateboard.

When he leaps off his skateboard, the skateboard moves in the opposite direction.
Maggie says that Newton's third law can be used to explain this.

(a) What does Newton's third law state?

....

....

(b) Use this to explain what happens to Karl and his skateboard.

....

....

(c) Karl sees the skateboard slow down and stop. He states: "That's because a force is needed to keep things moving at a steady speed." Explain what is wrong with this statement.

....

....

2 A pair of scooters (shown below) are about to set off on a race. The scooters are identical except for their drivers, and have engines which produce a thrust of 200 N.

Paul
mass 50 kg

Zahid
mass 75 kg

(a) Explain which of the scooters would you expect to be travelling fastest after 2 seconds.

....

(b) Paul and his scooter have a total mass of 90 kg.
Calculate the initial acceleration of Paul's scooter.

....

(c) Calculate the force produced when Paul brakes at the end of the race, decelerating at 5 m/s^2.

....

Section Two — Forces and Motion

Speed, Velocity and Acceleration

1. Amin is watching a greyhound race.

   (a) The winner finishes the 200 m race in 16 s. What was its average speed?

   ....

   (b) The second placed greyhound runs at an average speed of 11.9 m/s.
   How long does it take to complete the race?

   ....

2. Two aeroplanes in a flying display are shown below.

   140 m/s → ... 560 m ... ← 140 m/s

   A   B

   (a) The planes do not have the same velocity. Explain why this is the case.

   ....

   ....

   (b) If the planes were to continue at their current velocities,
   how long would it be before they collided?

   ....

   (c) To avoid the collision, plane A climbs away and plane B decelerates at a rate of 20 m/s².
   What will the velocity of plane B be after 2 seconds of deceleration?

   ....

   (d) A third aeroplane is on the runway. It needs to reach a takeoff speed of 120 m/s.
   If it takes 7.5 seconds to reach its takeoff speed from rest, what is its acceleration?

   ....

Distance-Time and Velocity-Time Graphs

1. A bullet is fired from a rifle at a shooting competition. It misses the target and is embedded in a straw bale. The graph shows the velocity of the bullet until the time it comes to rest in the straw.

   (a) The bullet takes 0.1 s to travel the 30 m to the bale.
   Use this information to work out the velocity A shown on the graph.

   ....

   (b) Calculate the deceleration of the bullet after it hits the straw bale.

   ....

   (c) How far does the bullet travel into the straw bale?

   ....

2. Two children are racing their trains on a wooden track.

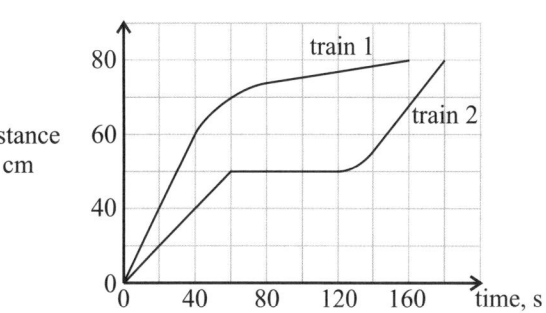

   (a) Between which times is train 2 stationary?

   ....

   (b) Both trains start at a steady speed. How do we know this?

   ....

   (c) Calculate the initial speed of the faster train.

   ....

   (d) When is train 1 decelerating?

   ....

Section Two — Forces and Motion

Resultant Force and Terminal Velocity

1. An aeroplane is launched from the deck of a ship. The diagram to the right shows this as viewed from directly above.

   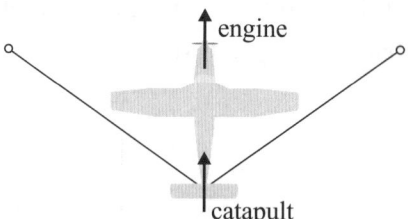

   The aeroplane has a mass of 2000 kg and its engine provides a force of 10 000 N. A catapult is used to help launch the plane, which provides 40 000 N of force.

   (a) What is the resultant force on the plane at the point of launch?

   ....

   (b) Use your answer to work out the acceleration of the plane as it is launched.

   ....

2. A skydiver jumps out of an aeroplane. Her weight is 700 N.

   (a) What force causes her to accelerate downwards?

   ....

   (b) After 10 s she is falling at a steady speed of 60 m/s. Calculate the force of air resistance that is acting on her.

   ....

   (c) She now opens her parachute, which increases the air resistance to 2000 N. Explain what immediately happens to her.

   ....

   ....

   (d) After falling with her parachute open for 5 s, she is travelling at a steady speed of 4 m/s. What is the air resistance force now?

   ....

Section Two — Forces and Motion

Stopping Distances for Cars

1. A van is driving along a road in the winter. The driver notices a sheep in the road and tries to stop.

   (a) What is meant by thinking distance?

   ....

   (b) Which two of the following will affect the driver's thinking distance? Underline your choices.

   Visibility   **Weight of vehicle**   **Condition of brakes**   **Tiredness of driver**

   (c) There are some icy patches on the road. What difference would it make to the thinking distance if the van was on an icy patch? Explain your answer.

   ....

2. The graph shows information about the stopping of a car tested on a dry track with an alert driver.

   (a) Explain why the thinking distance increases as the speed increases, despite the fact that the time taken for the driver to react remains constant.

   ....

   ....

   (b) What is the total stopping distance for the car travelling at 20 m/s?

   ....

   (c) If the speed doubles (from 15 m/s to 30 m/s) the braking distance more than doubles. Explain in terms of energy transformation why this is the case.

   ....

   ....

   ....

Section Two — Forces and Motion

Hooke's Law

1. A spring to be used in a child's toy is tested by applying forces to it in a laboratory.
   The original length of the spring is 5 cm. The table below shows four of the measurements taken.

force / N	1	2	3	4
length / cm	5.5	6.0	6.5	7.0
extension / cm				

   (a) Complete the table by calculating the extension for each force.

   (b) State Hooke's Law.

   ....

   ....

   (c) Use this, together with the information in the table, to predict a value of extension for 6 N.

   ....

   (d) Hooke's Law would predict an extension of 4 cm for the spring when a force of 8 N is applied. However, when measured, the extension for this force is 4.8 cm. Explain why the extension is greater than expected.

   ....

2. The graph shows the extension of a metal wire when large forces are applied to it.

   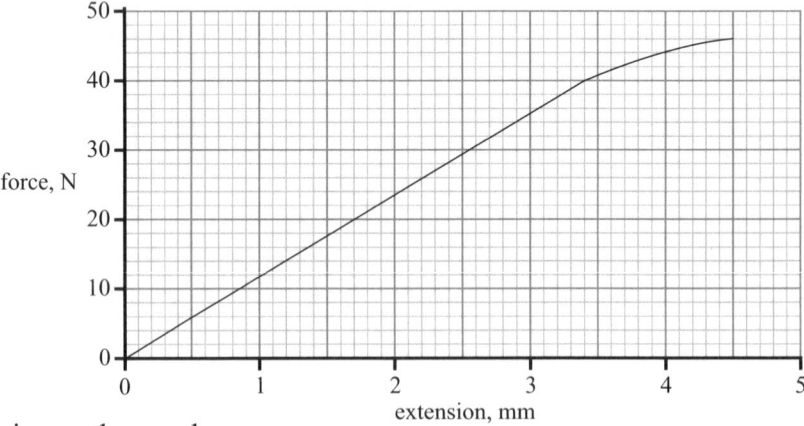

   (a) Mark the elastic limit of the wire on the graph.

   (b) What force is required to make the wire reach its elastic limit?

   ....

   (c) What would you expect to happen to the wire if a larger force than this were applied?

   ....

Boyle's Law: $P_1V_1 = P_2V_2$

1. The diagram below shows a canister of compressed air in a room.
   There are the same number of air particles in the canister as there are in the rest of the room.
   A piston at the base of the canister allows the air within to be further compressed.

   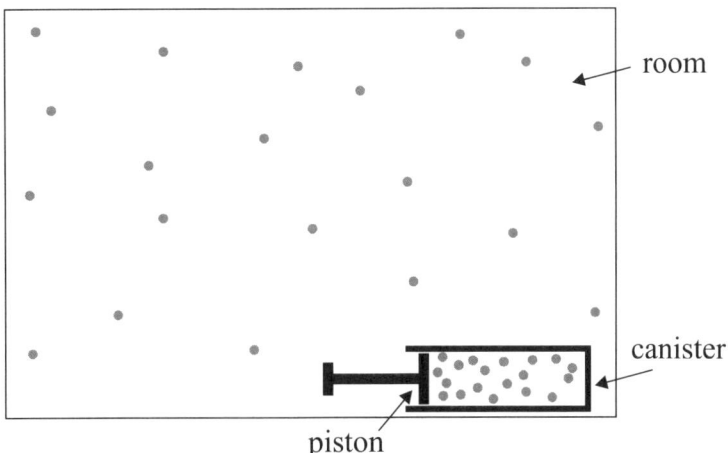

   (a) Use kinetic theory to explain why the gas in the canister is at a higher pressure than the gas in the room.

   ....

   ....

   (b) The piston in the canister is moved to the right until the pressure of the air doubles. The temperature of the air remains the same. What will happen to the volume?

   ....

   (c) Why is it important that the air has stayed at the same temperature?

   ....

2. This question concerns a gas manufactured for use as a propellant in aerosols.

   (a) A volume of 300 m³ of the gas held at a pressure of 1 atmosphere is to be compressed into a tank of volume 5 m³. What will the pressure of the gas in this tank be?

   ....

   (b) The gas is then transferred, under the same high pressure, into aerosol cans of volume 50 cm³. What volume would the gas from one aerosol can occupy if it were released back into the atmosphere (i.e. at 1 atmosphere pressure)?

   ....

Section Two — Forces and Motion

Forces and Motion Mini-Exam (1)

1. A ball is dropped and bounces up. After a while it stops bouncing and rests on the ground.

   (a) Add labels to the ball in each diagram to show the forces acting on the ball at each position.

   ball at top of bounce ○

   ball resting on the ground
   ○

   (b) The ball has a mass of 800 g. Calculate the weight of the ball.
   Assume the gravitational field strength is 10 N/kg.

   ....

   (c) The ball is thrown at a wall. It reaches the wall in 3.5 seconds.
   If the ball is moving at 2.2 m/s, how far does it travel to reach the wall?

   ....

2. The graph below is drawn for Geraldine's radio controlled car.
   The car is initially driven away from Geraldine, then back towards her.

   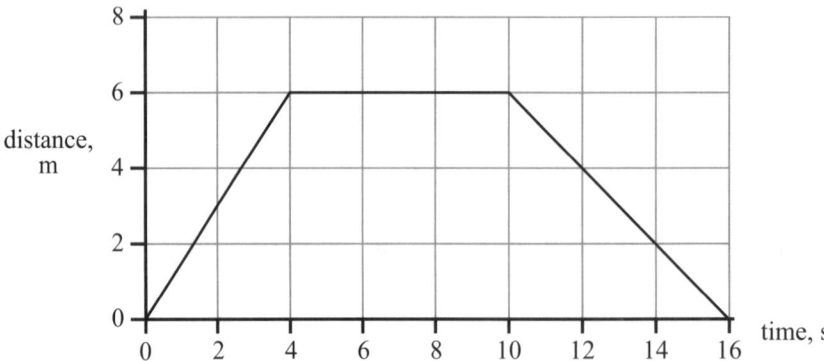

   (a) The car stopped during its journey. How do we know this, and how long did it stop for?

   ....

   ....

   (b) Calculate the speed of the car as it moves away from Geraldine.

   ....

   (c) How do we know that the car was moving more slowly when it came back to Geraldine?

   ....

Section Two — Forces and Motion

Forces and Motion Mini-Exam (2)

3 Tariq's bicycle has a puncture. He uses a lever to remove the tyre.

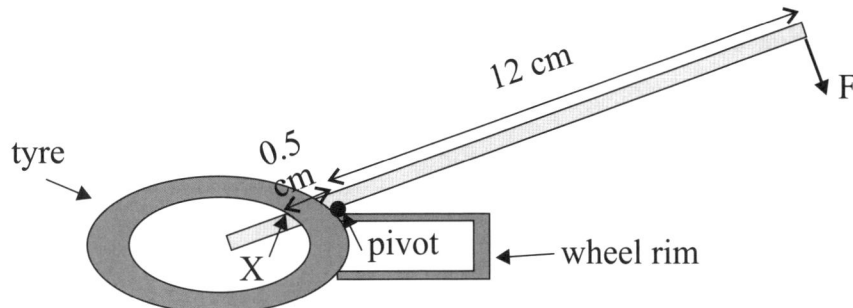

(a) If Tariq pushes with a force of 50 N at point F on the diagram, what clockwise moment will be created about the pivot?

....

(b) Use your answer to work out the force exerted on the tyre by the tyre lever at point X.

....

(c) Tariq needs to inflate the tyre to a pressure of 5 atmospheres.
The total volume of the inflated tyre is 400 cm^3.
What volume of air at normal atmospheric pressure needs to be pumped into the tyre?

....

(d) (i) Tariq later makes an emergency stop. Name the force, between the road and the tyres, which enables him to stop and state the direction in which it acts.

....

(ii) It takes Tariq 2 seconds to reduce his speed from 4 m/s to 0 m/s.
What is Tariq's acceleration?

....

(e) A friend observes Tariq cycling around a roundabout.
The friend states: "Tariq is cycling in a circle with a constant velocity of 5 m/s."
Explain why the statement cannot be correct.

....

....

Section Two — Forces and Motion

Forces and Motion Mini-Exam (3)

4   The diagram below shows a cross section through a toy gun, which is designed to fire small plastic pellets. The spring is extended 6 cm when the gun is loaded and the pellet is held in a cradle. When the trigger is pulled the spring is released, firing the pellet.

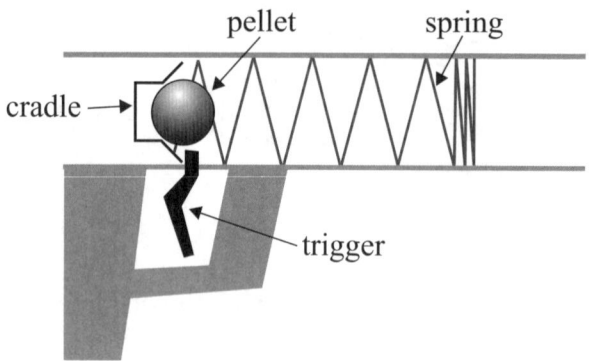

(a) (i) The force the spring exerts on the pellet when the trigger is pulled is 4 N. The mass of the pellet is 75 g. Calculate the initial acceleration of the pellet.

....

(ii) A different pellet is loaded into the gun. The spring is released and applies the same force as before, 4 N. If the mass of the new pellet is 125 g, what will be the initial acceleration given to the pellet?

....

(b) The pellet is accelerated by the spring for 0.64 seconds.
The average acceleration in this time is 20 m/s^2.
Use this information to deduce the velocity of the pellet as it leaves the gun.

....

(c) (You only need to do this question if you're doing the **Edexcel** syllabus.)

A new version of the gun has a longer barrel, enabling the spring to be extended by 12 cm. The spring used obeys Hooke's Law and a 12 cm extension is within its elastic limit. What force would you expect to be exerted on the pellet now? Explain your answer.

....

....

Section Three — Waves

Waves — Basic Principles

1. The diagram shows a picture of a water wave.
   Four distances are marked A, B C and D on the diagram.

   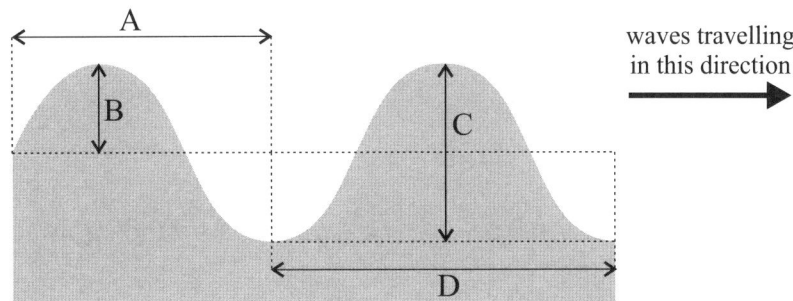

   (a) Which of the distances A, B C or D shows:

   (i) the wavelength of the wave. ....

   (ii) the amplitude of the wave. ....

   (b) The wave in the diagram is travelling from left to right.
   Which one of the following statements is true about the wave? Tick the correct answer.

   ☐ **The water molecules vibrate left to right.**

   ☐ **The water moves from left to right.**

   ☐ **Energy is transferred from left to right.**

   (c) The water wave shown is a transverse wave. Give one other example of a transverse wave.

   ....

   (d) Explain the difference between transverse and longitudinal waves.

   ....

   ....

   (e) In the space below draw a diagram of a longitudinal wave and label:
   (i) compressions, (ii) rarefactions, (iii) one wavelength.

Section Three — Waves

Sound Waves

1. This question is about sound.

    (a) The table shows the speed of sound in various substances.

substance	density, g/cm³	speed, m/s
air	0.001	330
water	1.0	1400
iron	7.9	5000

    (i) Explain in terms of particles why sound travels faster through water than air.

    ....

    ....

    (ii) Why can't sound travel through a vacuum?

    ....

    (b) Noise pollution can be unpleasant and harmful.

    (i) Suggest three ways to reduce the effects of noise.

    ....

    (ii) Use the graph to describe what may happen if your hearing is damaged.

    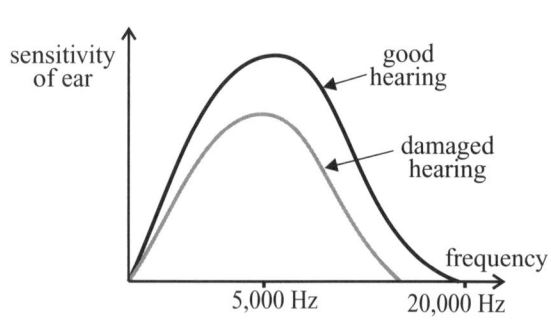

    ....

    ....

    (c) Quiet sounds can be amplified to louder sounds using an amplifier.
    Complete the diagram below by drawing a possible output wave from the amplifier.

    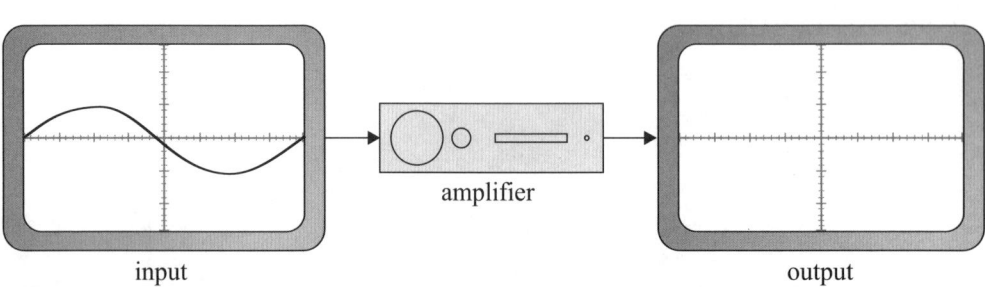

Section Three — Waves

Ultrasound

1. This question is about ultrasound.

    (a) Circle the correct answer in each case.

    (i) Ultrasound refers to sounds with a very high

    wavelength **amplitude** **frequency** **speed**

    (ii) These sound waves are produced by vibrations of above

    20 Hz **20 kHz** **1000Hz** **20 000kHz**

    (iii) 1 kHz is equal to

    1000 vib/hour **1 vib/sec** **1000 vib/min** **1000 vib/sec**

    (b) The following sentences explain how bats use ultrasound as a form of echolocation. Write numbers in the boxes to show the correct order of the sentences.

    ☐ The echoes are detected by the bat's big ears.

    ☐ They send out high-pitched squeaks.

    ☐ The bat processes the signal, and forms a "sonic" image of its surroundings.

    ☐ The sound waves reflect off objects (echo).

    (c) Ultrasound has many practical uses in medicine and in industry.

    (i) Write down two uses of ultrasound in industry.

    ....

    (ii) Explain in detail how ultrasound is used to study the development of an unborn foetus.

    ....

    ....

    ....

    (iii) Give one other medical use of ultrasound.

    ....

Section Three — Waves

Questions on the Speed of Sound

1. In these questions you may need to know:
   the speed of sound in air is 330 m/s and in water is 1400 m/s;
   the speed of electromagnetic waves in air is 3×10^8 m/s.

   (a) Kat bangs a tuning fork. It produces a note of 250 Hz.
   Calculate the wavelength of the sound wave.

   ....

   (b) Microwaves used in microwave ovens have a wavelength of 10 cm. Calculate their frequency.

   ....

   (c) Captain Will is measuring the depth of the ocean. His ship sends out a high frequency sound wave, which reflects off the sea bed. The time between sending out and receiving the signal is 1.2 seconds. Calculate the depth of the ocean.

   ....

   (d) A humming bird can flap its wings 3000 times in a minute.
   Calculate the frequency (in Hertz), and the time period (in seconds) of one flap.

   ....

   (e) When a wave passes from one substance to another, its wavelength and speed will change, but its frequency stays the same. The diagram is of an ultrasonic scanner testing for cracks in metal castings.

   speed of waves = 5000 m/s
   wavelength = 0.05 m

   (i) Use the information to calculate the frequency of the wave.

   ....

   (ii) Will the wavelength of the wave be greater in iron or air? Explain your answer.

   ....

   ....

Section Three — Waves

Reflection: a Property of all Waves

1. The diagram below shows a ray of light hitting a plane mirror.

   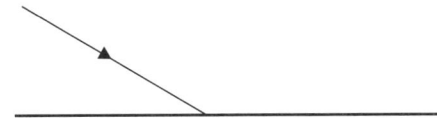

   (a) Complete the diagram to show the reflection of the ray.

   (b) If the angle of incidence is 35°, what will the angle of reflection be?

   ....

2. Electromagnetic radio waves are detected by a satellite dish.

   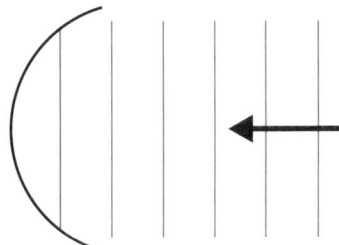

   (a) Complete the diagram to show how the waves are reflected at the surface of the dish.

   (b) Mark the diagram with an X where the detector should be placed.

3. Dave stands before a mirror and sees the image of a ball.

   (a) Complete the ray diagram to show: (i) the light rays reflected in the mirror;
   (ii) the position of the virtual image of the ball.

   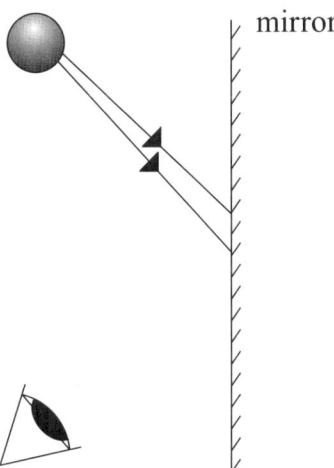

   (b) The ball is 0.5 m away from the mirror. How far is the ball from its image?

   ....

Section Three — Waves

Refraction: a Property of all Waves

1. The diagram below shows a light wave entering a glass block.

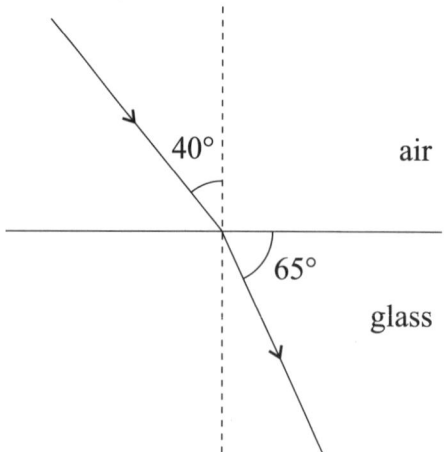

(a) The diagram shows a light wave changing direction as it enters a glass block. What name is given to this effect?

....

(b) What is the value of the angle of incidence in the air?

....

(c) What is the value of the angle of refraction in the glass?

....

(d) Other than its direction, name one property of the light wave that changes when it enters the glass block.

....

(e) A different light ray enters the glass block. Complete the diagram below to show the path the light ray will take when it enters the glass block.

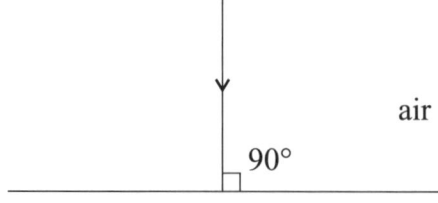

Section Three — Waves

Refraction: Two Special Cases

1 Refraction occurs when waves enter a different medium.

   (a) Complete the diagram below to show the paths of the two light rays through the glass block.

   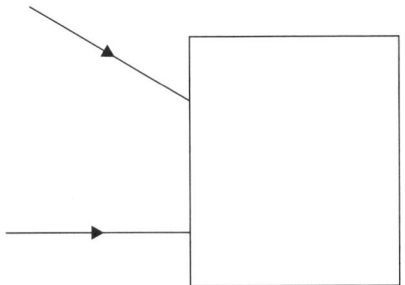

   (b) Explain why white light splits into the colours of the rainbow when it passes through a prism.

   ....

   ....

2 The critical angle for glass is 42°.
   On each diagram below, draw the path the light takes after entering the semicircular block.

   (a) Incident angle = 20°

   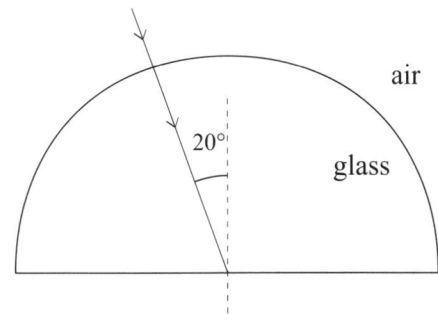

   (b) Incident angle = 42°

   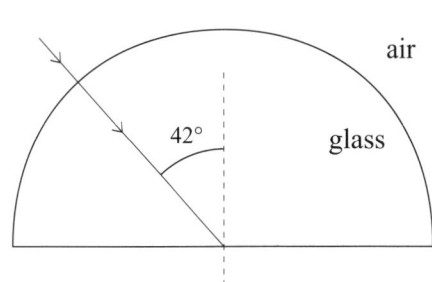

   (c) Incident angle = 60°

   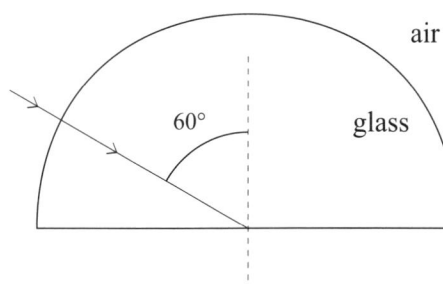

Section Three — Waves

Uses of Total Internal Reflection

1. Some periscopes use total internal reflection to work.
   The diagram below shows the path of a ray of light as it passes through one of these periscopes.

   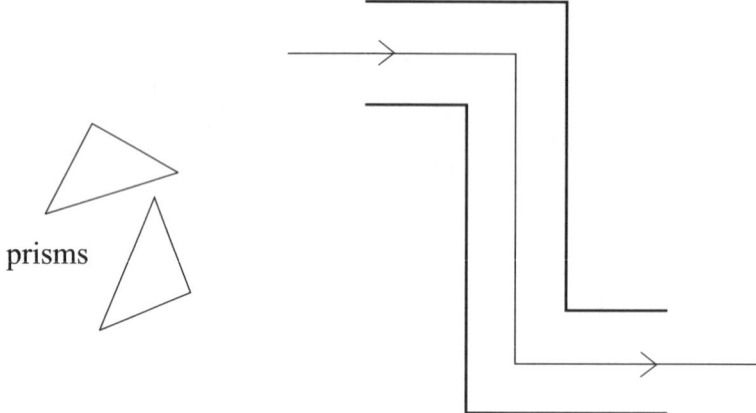

   (a) Complete the diagram by adding the position of the two prisms needed to make the periscope work. The prisms can be rotated from the positions shown.

   (b) Name one other device that uses totally internally reflecting prisms to work.

   ....

2. Optical fibres make use of total internal reflection to transmit information over long distances.

   (a) State three advantages of using optical fibres over electrical cables.

   ....

   ....

   ....

   (b) Optical fibres are also used to make endoscopes for keyhole surgery. This is very useful in knee operations. Use the diagram below to help explain how the endoscope works.

   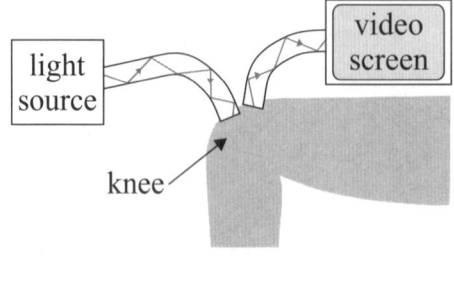

   ....

   ....

Section Three — Waves

Digital and Analogue Signals

1. Information can be transmitted as analogue or digital signals.

   (a) The diagram below shows an analogue signal.
   In the box on the right, draw an equivalent digital signal.

   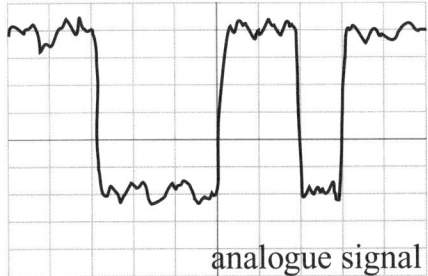
   analogue signal

   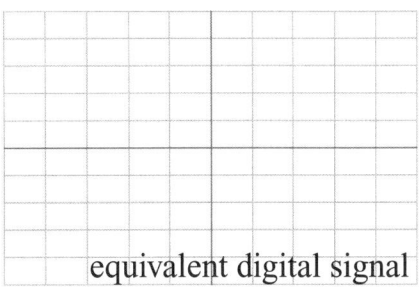
   equivalent digital signal

   (b) Explain the difference between the two signals.

   ....

   ....

   (c) Give two examples of:

   (i) analogue devices;

   ....

   (ii) digital devices.

   ....

   (d) Give two ways that either of the signals shown above
   could be transmitted over long distances.

   ....

   ....

   (e) Digital signal tends to be of better quality than analogue signals.
   Give one other advantage using digital rather than analogue signals to transmit information.

   ....

Section Three — Waves

Diffraction: a Property of all Waves

1   This question is about diffraction.
    Diffraction is the spreading out of waves when they pass through a gap or past an object.

    Complete the diagrams below to show the path of the waves.

    (a)   (b)   (c)

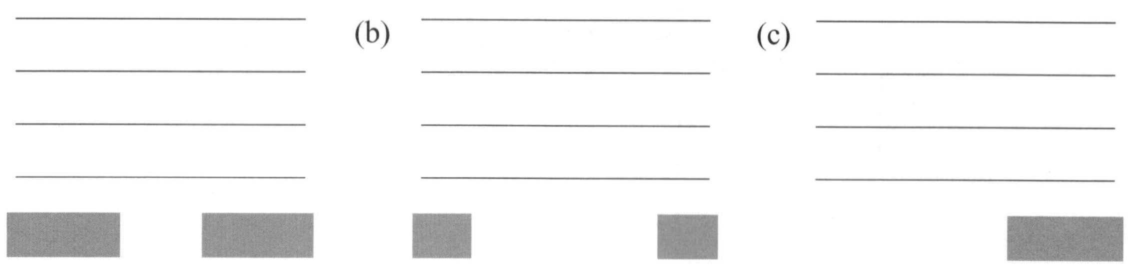

2   The diffraction of waves affects many everyday situations.

    (a) Isabel is listening to music with her window open. Her friend Josie is walking past and notices that the music sounds muffled. By considering the effect of frequency on diffraction, explain why she can't hear the high-pitched parts of the music.

    ....

    ....

    (b) Complete the diagram below to show which radio station the house behind the hill will detect most easily.

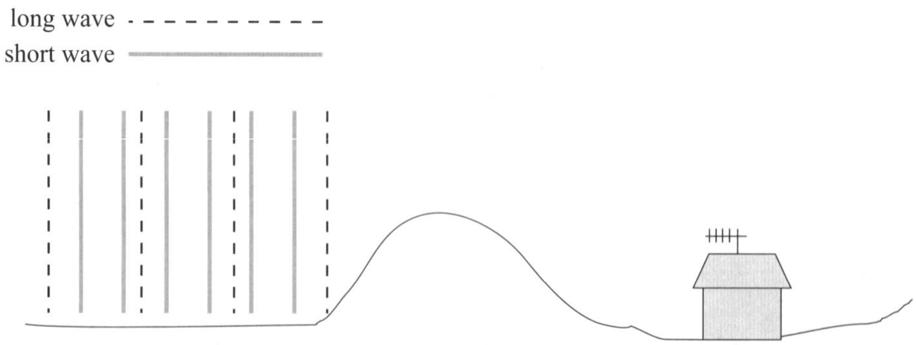

        long wave - - - - - - - - -
        short wave ─────────

    (c) Diffraction of sound allows us to hear around corners.
        Sound and light both travel as waves. Explain why it is not possible to see around corners.

    ....

    ....

Section Three — Waves

The Electromagnetic Spectrum

1 This question is about the electromagnetic (EM) spectrum.

   (a) Fill in the gaps to complete the part of the EM spectrum shown below.

   microwaves .... X-rays

   (b) Which of the EM waves above have the highest frequency?

   ....

   (c) Tick the appropriate box to show whether each of the statements below is true or false.

True	False	Statement
☐	☐	EM waves can cause heating when absorbed.
☐	☐	EM waves are longitudinal waves.
☐	☐	EM waves cannot travel through a vacuum.
☐	☐	Some EM waves can cause alternating currents to flow in conductors.
☐	☐	EM waves can be reflected but not refracted or diffracted.
☐	☐	Some EM waves can ionise living cells and cause cancer.
☐	☐	EM waves all travel at the speed of sound.

2 There are different types of radio wave, but they all are used for communication.

   (a) Write short, medium or long to show the wavelengths of the radio signals on the diagram.

   (b) Write in typical values for the wavelength of each type of wave.

Section Three — Waves

Microwaves and Infrared

1   Microwave radiation is produced when a current flows through a conductor.

   (a)   Microwave ovens can be used to cook food.

      (i)   Explain how microwave ovens work.

      ....

      ....

      (ii) A traditional oven uses infrared radiation.
            Suggest two advantages of using a microwave oven.

      ....

      ....

   (b) Give another use for microwaves.

      ....

   (c) Explain why certain frequency microwaves can be dangerous to people.

      ....

      ....

2   Infrared radiation is used for TV remote controls. Jake shows Peter than he can change the TV channel by pointing the remote control at a mirror on the opposite wall.

   (a) What property of EM rays has Jake demonstrated?

      ....

   (b) Peter places a dull black piece of card over the mirror and tries to change channel in the same way. Explain what will happen now and why.

      ....

      ....

   (c) Give another use of infrared radiation.

      ....

Section Three — Waves

Visible and UV Light, X-Rays and Gamma Rays

1. Ultraviolet light and X-rays are next to each other in the electromagnetic spectrum.

    (a) State one difference and one similarity between ultraviolet light and X-rays.

    ....

    (b) Write **X-rays**, **UV radiation**, **visible light** or **gamma radiation** to show what each statement below is describing.

    (i) Used to show hidden security markings.　　　　..............................

    (ii) Used to prolong the shelf life of fresh foods.　　　..............................

    (iii) Has a typical wavelength of 5×10^{-7} m.　　　..............................

    (iv) Used in hospitals to treat cancer.　　　..............................

2. The diagram shows an X-ray shadow image of a hand.

    (a) Explain why the bones show on the photographic plate, but the flesh of the hand does not.

    ....

    ....

    (b) Suggest what has caused the white band across one of the fingers.

    ....

    (c) Radiographers operate X-ray machines in hospitals.

    (i) Suggest two safety precautions they must take to avoid the risks associated with exposure to X-rays.

    ....

    (ii) Give two uses for gamma rays in hospitals.

    ....

Section Three — Waves

Seismic Waves

1. Earthquakes cause shock waves, called S-waves and P-waves, which travel through the Earth.

    (a) Which are the fastest, P-waves or S-waves?

    ....

    (b) The diagram shows the paths of P-waves through the Earth.

    (i) On the diagram, complete the path of wave X.

    (ii) P-waves don't reach zone Z. Look at diagram and explain why.

    ....

    ....

    (iii) Explain why the waves change direction as they pass through Earth.

    ....

    ....

    (c) The diagram shows the paths of S-waves through the Earth.

    (i) S-waves don't reach zone Y. Name the layer of the earth that S-waves will not pass through.

    ....

    (ii) Why don't the S-waves pass through this layer?

    ....

    ....

Section Three — Waves

Earth's Structure

1. Seismologists learn about the structure of the Earth by studying shock waves from earthquakes. For each observation below, state what this tells us about the structure of the Earth.

    (a) The deeper seismic waves go into the mantle, the faster they travel.

    ....

    (b) The density of the rocks in the Earth's crust is less than half the average density of the Earth.

    ....

    (c) S-waves cannot travel through the outer core.

    ....

    (d) P-waves change direction abruptly about halfway through the Earth.

    ....

2. The Earth has a dense core, and a crust made of large, slowly moving plates.

    (a) Explain in detail what causes the movement of these plates.

    ....

    ....

    ....

    (b) It is believed that the dense core is made of nickel and iron.

    (i) What evidence is used to determine the density of the Earth?

    ....

    ....

    (ii) State what evidence suggests the core is made of nickel and iron.

    ....

    ....

Section Three — Waves

Evidence for Plate Tectonics

1. Vertical boreholes were drilled in three different continents to study the order of the rocks. The borehole results are shown below.

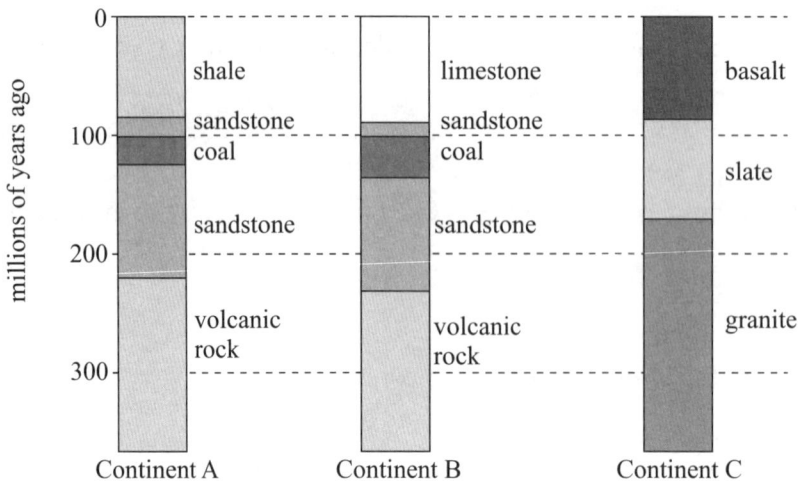

(a) Which two continents do the results suggest were once joined as part of a supercontinent?

....

(b) Explain your answer to part (a).

....

(c) Roughly when do the two continents appear to have started to split and move apart?

....

2. The theory of continental drift was proposed in 1915 by Alfred Wegener.
He stated that the continents were once joined, and have slowly drifted apart.

(a) How does studying a map of the continents suggest that they were once joined?

....

(b) What is "Pangaea"?

....

(c) Explain how fossil evidence supports the theory of continental drift.

....

....

Section Three — Waves

Plate Boundaries

1   Read the passage and answer the questions below.

> *1*   Sea-floor spreading is the process whereby two plates move apart, and molten magma rises up at a plate boundary forming new rock (basalt). This type of boundary between separating plates is called a constructive boundary.
>
> The evidence for Sea-floor spreading can be found by comparing the age and
> *5*   the magnetic properties of rocks at different distances from the diverging ridge.
>
> Bands of rock with opposite magnetic polarity occur in the ocean basins. This is because the Earth's magnetic field swaps direction every 500 000 years or so. This behaviour is recorded by the basalt, because it contains magnetic materials, which aligned themselves with the Earth's magnetic field when the basalt
> *10* solidified. As new basalt forms the old rock is pushed to the side, producing bands of alternating magnetic polarity.

(a) Give an example of an oceanic ridge where sea-floor spreading occurs.

    ....

(b) Suggest why the boundary in line 3 is called a constructive boundary.

    ....

(c) What is meant by the "diverging ridge" in line 5?

    ....

(d) What element does basalt contain to account for its magnetic behaviour?

    ....

(e) What factors provide the best evidence for sea-floor spreading?

    ....

    ....

Section Three — Waves

Waves Mini-Exam (1)

1. Waves can be of one of two types — transverse or longitudinal.

    (a) Say whether each of the following are transverse or longitudinal waves.

    (i) sound ....

    (ii) gamma rays ....

    (iii) waves on a string ....

    (iv) seismic P-waves ....

    (b) Explain how a longitudinal wave differs from a transverse wave.

    ....

    ....

2. The diagram below shows a drum being hit.
    This causes the skin to vibrate, which sets up vibrations in the air molecules around it.

    (a) On the diagram show:

    (i) the position of the compressions and rarefactions,

    (ii) a distance represented by one wavelength.

    The drummer now tightens the skin using screws on the side of the drum.

    (b) How would you expect this to change the sound produced by the drum?

    ....

    (c) Describe how could you redraw the diagram to show this change.

    ....

Section Three — Waves

Waves Mini-Exam (2)

3   Sound waves are vibrations of air particles. They cannot pass through a vacuum.

   (a) Describe, with the aid of a diagram, an experiment to show that sound cannot travel through a vacuum.

   ....

   ....

   (b) Use the diagram below to calculate the speed of sound in air, using the recorded time interval between hitting the drum and hearing the echo from the wall. Show your working.

   200 m

   time interval between drumbeat and echo = 1.25 s

   ....

   ....

4   This question is about radio waves. Radio waves travel at 3×10^8 m/s through air.

   (a) Radio Roary transmits signals with a wavelength of 1.5 km.
       Calculate its frequency. Show your working.

   ....

   ....

   (b) Radio X broadcasts at a frequency of 1×10^8 Hz. How does its wavelength compare with that of Radio Roary? Show clearly how you arrived at your answer.

   ....

   ....

Section Three — Waves

Waves Mini-Exam (3)

5   During a thunderstorm, a flash of lightning is seen, followed a few moments later by thunder.

   (a) Explain why you see the flash of lightning before you hear the clap of thunder.

   ....

   ....

   (b) As a storm moves further away, explain what happens to the time interval between the lightning and the thunder.

   ....

   ....

6   The diagram shows light incident on a bicycle reflector.

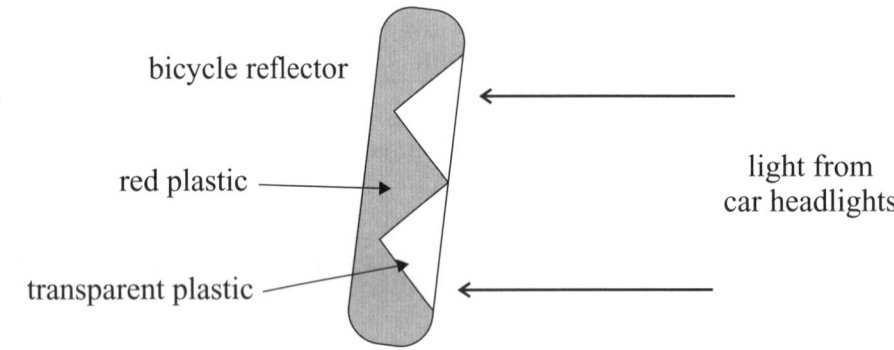

   (a) Continue the paths of the two light rays to show what happens to them when they hit the reflector.

   (b) Complete the diagram below to show how light passes through an optical fibre.

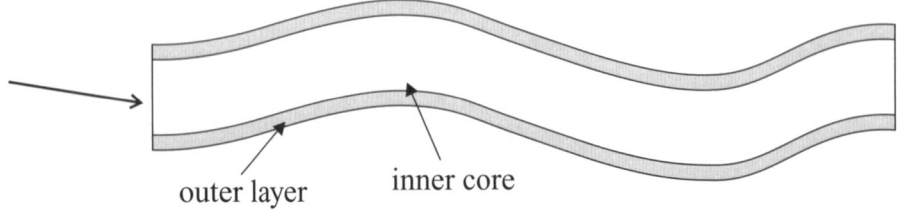

   (c) Explain how optical fibres work.

   ....

   ....

Section Three — Waves

Waves Mini-Exam (4)

7   The following sentences about analogue and digital signals are incorrect.
    Rewrite them so that they are correct.

    (a) Analogue signals are those in which amplitude, speed and frequency vary continuously.

    ....

    ....

    (b) Digital signals can be sent as EM waves, but analogue ones are transmitted by electrical signals in cables.

    ....

    ....

    (c) Analogue signals are less prone to interference called "sounds" and so produce better quality signals than digital ones.

    ....

    ....

8   Use the diagram below to explain how the Himalayas were formed.
    Include diagrams if it will help your explanation.

    Indian and Asian plates, prior to collision.

    ....

    ....

    ....

    ....

Section Three — Waves

Section Four — Outer Space

The Planets

1. The Solar System consists of planets which orbit the Sun.
   Venus and Mars are two of the inner planets.

   (a) These two planets can be seen using only the naked eye.
   Explain how the planets can be seen even though they do not produce light of their own.

   ....

   ....

   (b) Name the other two inner planets.

   ....

   (c) Jupiter is one of the outer planets. What can you say about the length of a Jupiter year compared with the length of an Earth year? Explain your answer.

   ....

   ....

2. The Earth has an average distance from the Sun of 150 million kilometres.
   There are two imaginary planets, planet A and planet B, which have the same mass as the Earth.
   Planet A is 75 million kilometres from the Sun.

   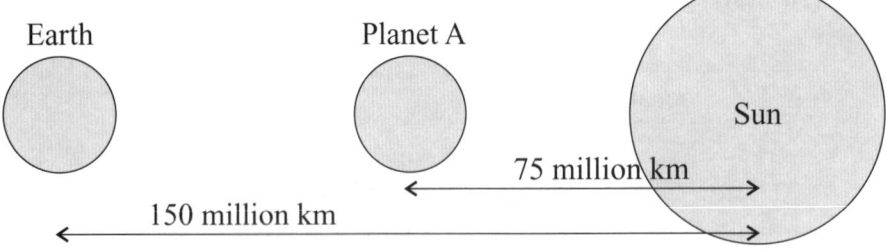

   (a) The Sun exerts a gravitational pull on both planets in the diagram. What would be the size of the force exerted on planet A, compared to the size of the force exerted on the Earth?

   ....

   (b) The force of gravitational attraction between the Sun and planet B is one ninth of that between the Sun and the Earth. How far is planet B from the Sun?

   ....

Moons, Meteorites, Asteroids and Comets

1. The Moon is a satellite of the Earth. It orbits the Earth once every twenty-eight days.

   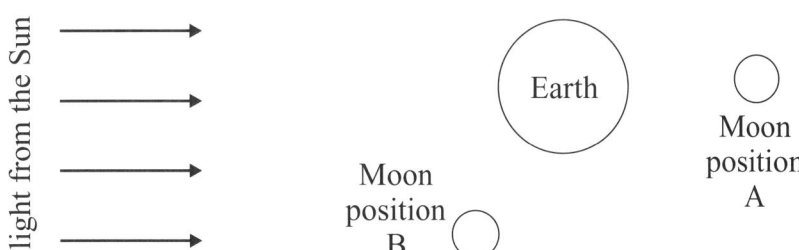

   (a) When the Moon is in position A, it appears as a full moon from the Earth. Explain why.

   ....

   ....

   (b) Describe how the Moon would appear from the Earth seven days later.

   ....

   (c) How would the Moon appear from the Earth when it is in position B?

   ....

   (d) The same side of the Moon always faces the Earth.
   Use this fact to explain how long a "day" is on the Moon.

   ....

   ....

   ....

2. Asteroids are randomly sized lumps of rock that orbit the Sun. Meteors are asteroids that have been knocked out of their orbit causing them to travel towards the Earth.

   (a) Describe what happens to most small meteors when they enter the Earth's atmosphere.

   ....

   (b) What might happen if the meteor was very large?

   ....

Section Four — Outer Space

Satellites

1. The diagram shows the orbits of two types of satellite, a polar orbit and a geostationary orbit.

   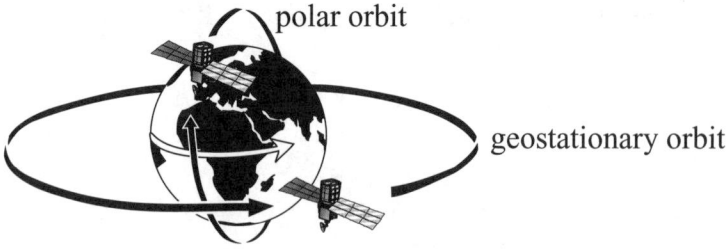

   (a) A satellite in a stable Earth orbit moves at a constant speed in a circular orbit because there is a single force acting on it.

   (i) What is the name of this force?

   ....

   (ii) Explain in which of the orbits shown this force would be bigger.

   ....

   ....

   (b) Communications satellites are usually geostationary satellites.

   (i) Explain what is meant by the term "geostationary satellite".

   ....

   ....

   (ii) What is the advantage of a geostationary orbit for communications satellites?

   ....

   (iii) How long does it take for this type of satellite to complete one orbit?

   ....

   (c) Give one use of a satellite in polar orbit.

   ....

   (d) Explain why a satellite does not need to have a streamlined shape, even though it is moving very rapidly.

   ....

   ....

Section Four — Outer Space

Searching for Life on Other Planets

1   There are two ways in which we might communicate with life from elsewhere in the universe.

   (a) One way is for that life to detect that we are on the Earth. Name three kinds of signal that we produce on Earth that might be picked up by a being on another planet.

   ....

   (b) How quickly are these signals travelling through space?

   ....

   (c) The other way of communicating is for us to detect signals that reach the Earth from outer space. A scientist detects radio signals of a range of wavelengths, coming from another galaxy. Are the signals likely to be from an alien race? Explain your answer.

   ....

   ....

2   Space exploration using robot buggies has been limited to the Moon, Mars and Europa, one of the moons of Jupiter.

   the surface of Mars

   (a) Give two different kinds of information a robot might send to the Earth for scientists to study.

   ....

   (b) It is unlikely that there are organisms alive today on Mars, but scientists still want to study rock samples from the Martian surface. Suggest how these samples might provide evidence for the existence of life on other planets.

   ....

   (c) Spacecraft and robot probes are extremely expensive. Explain how a scientist might look for life on other planets, without sending any equipment into space.

   ....

   ....

Section Four — Outer Space

The Universe

1   Stars are formed from clouds of dust which spiral in together.

   (a) The dust cloud is compressed so much that it gets very hot.
       What process is started by this very high temperature?

       ....

   (b) Explain briefly how planets are formed.

       ....

       ....

2   The Sun is one of many millions of stars in our galaxy.

   (a) (i) Name our galaxy.   ....

       (ii) Describe the position of the Sun in our galaxy.

            ....

   (b) Approximately how many galaxies are there in the Universe? Underline the correct answer.

       less than one million   more than a million but less than a billion   more than a billion

3   Towards the end of its life, a star may become a neutron star and eventually a black hole.

   (a) In what circumstances will a star at the end of its life turn into a black hole?

       ....

   (b) Explain why it is called a black hole.

       ....

       ....

   (c) Astronomers have detected X-rays which come from close to black holes.
       How are these X-rays produced?

       ....

Section Four — Outer Space

The Life Cycle of Stars

1. Astronomers have identified six main stages in the life and death of a small star such as our Sun. The diagram shows these stages in picture form and gives you the names of three of the six stages.

Stage 1	Stage 2	Stage 3	Stage 4	Stage 5	Stage 6
clouds of dust and gas		main sequence star	red giant		

(a) What does the cloud of dust and gas at stage 1 turn into at stage 2?

....

(b) Explain what happens in stage 2.

....

....

(c) At stage 3, the star is a main sequence star. The star gives off huge amounts of heat and light energy. Explain how such a large amount of energy is produced.

....

....

(d) At stage 4 the star is known as a Red Giant. Why has the surface of the star become red?

....

(e) What are the names of the stars in stages 5 and 6?

Stage 5: .... Stage 6: ....

(f) We find heavier elements on the Earth which are not produced in the life cycle of a small star. Explain how this can be the case.

....

....

Section Four — Outer Space

The Origin of the Universe

1. This question looks at one of the main pieces of evidence to support the Big Bang Theory.

    (a) The siren from an ambulance moving towards you sounds to be a higher pitch than it would if the ambulance were stationary. What is the name of this effect?

    ....

    (b) What would you hear if the ambulance moved away from you while sounding its siren?

    ....

    (c) A light source produces all the frequencies of the visible spectrum. When the light is passed through cool hydrogen gas, the spectrum is crossed by a series of dark lines, the absorption spectrum of hydrogen. The diagram shows what this might look like.

    red ⎯⎯⎯⎯⎯⎯⎯⎯⎯⎯⎯⎯⎯⎯⎯⎯ violet

    (i) When light from a distant galaxy is observed, the absorption spectrum is different in one important way. What is this important difference?

    ....

    (ii) What is this effect known as?

    ....

    (iii) What does this suggest about the distant galaxies?

    ....

2. Another piece of evidence for the Big Bang Theory is background radiation. This background radiation is not the same as the radioactive background count that affects a Geiger counter.

    (a) What kind of radiation is the background radiation left over from the Big Bang?

    ....

    (b) Where is this background radiation observed to come from?

    ....

    (c) What happens to this radiation as the universe expands and cools?

    ....

Section Four — Outer Space

The Origin and Future of the Universe

1. This diagram shows how the universe is thought to have changed in the past, and one possible way it might develop in the future.

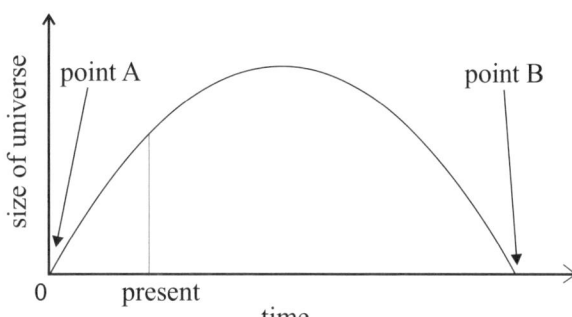

(a) What is the name for the event that happened at point A?

....

(b) Briefly describe the size and temperature of the universe at point A.

....

(c) What is the current estimate for the age of the universe? How has this age been calculated?

....

....

(d) What happens to the universe in the future depends on the total mass of the universe.

   (i) If the possibility shown in the diagram turns out to be correct, briefly describe what will happen at point B.

   ....

   ....

   (ii) If there is not enough mass in the universe, the event shown at point B will not take place. What would happen to the universe instead?

   ....

   (iii) Explain why it is difficult to estimate the total mass of the universe.

   ....

   ....

Section Four — Outer Space

Outer Space Mini-Exam (1)

1. Two different satellites can be seen through a telescope. Satellite A appears to be stationary in the sky. Satellite B appears to move fairly quickly through the sky in a straight line.

    (a) Describe the different types of orbit followed by satellites A and B.
    You may use a diagram if you wish.

    ....

    ....

    ....

    (b) Which of the two might be visible without a telescope?

    ....

    (c) State one possible use for satellite A, and one possible use for satellite B.

    (i) Satellite A   ....

    (ii) Satellite B   ....

2. The nine planets of the solar system orbit the Sun.

    (a) Jupiter is one of the outer planets. Name two other outer planets.

    ....

    (b) Comets are also in orbit around the Sun.
    State two ways in which the orbit of a comet is different to the orbit of a planet.

    1. ....

    2. ....

    (c) Planets are seen because they reflect light from the Sun.
    How does the Sun produce its own light?

    ....

Section Four — Outer Space

Outer Space Mini-Exam (2)

3   The life cycle of a large star is shown in the diagram. Some of the stages are named.

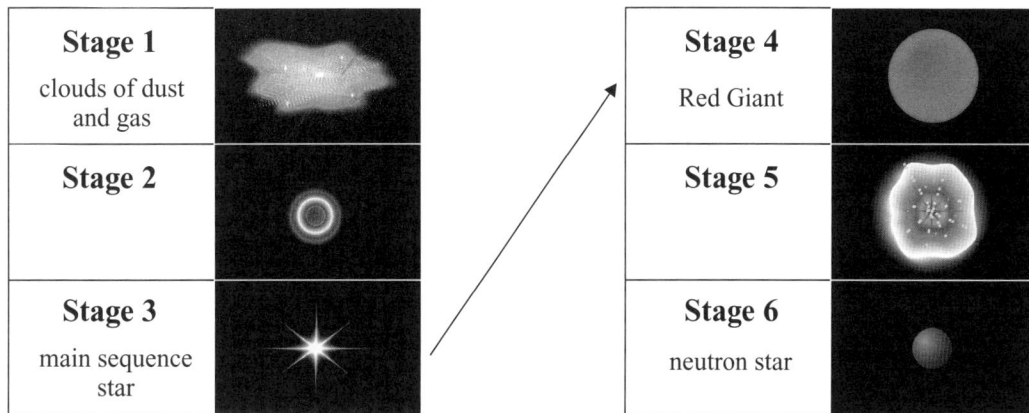

(a) What reactions are taking place inside the star during the Red Giant stage?

....

(b) Eventually the Red Giant explodes. What is stage 5 called?

....

(c) The explosion leaves a very dense core of matter called a neutron star. Explain what may happen to a very large neutron star.

....

(d) Describe what happens to the outer dust and debris of the exploding star.

....

4   The diagram shows what the Milky Way galaxy would look like when viewed from another part of the Universe.

(a) What does the shape of the galaxy tell us about the way it is moving?

....

(b) Light travels at a speed of 300 000 km each second. How far away is the Sun from the Earth if it takes light 500 seconds to travel from the Sun to the Earth?

....

Section Four — Outer Space

Outer Space Mini-Exam (3)

5   Using a telescope, an astronomer on Earth can see that Jupiter has four moons.

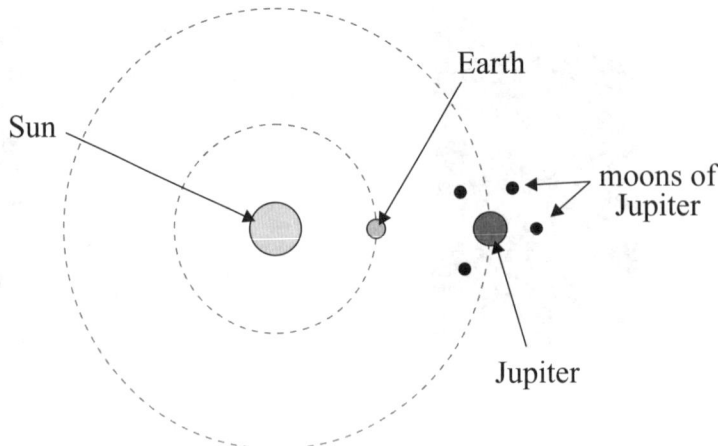

(a) Explain why the moons can be seen from the Earth.

   ....

(b) What would the shape of the moons be when observed from the Earth?

   ....

(c) What keeps the moons in orbit around the planet?

   ....

(d) Several planets have been detected in other solar systems.
    Explain why these planets are very difficult to observe.

   ....

   ....

(e) One way in which scientists are looking for evidence of life elsewhere in the universe
    is to investigate the conditions on other planets using observations from the Earth.
    What could light reflected from the surface of a planet tell us about the conditions there?

   ....

   ....

Section Four — Outer Space

Section Five — Energy

Energy Transfer

1. The diagram below shows a table lamp, which has been plugged into an electrical socket and switched on.

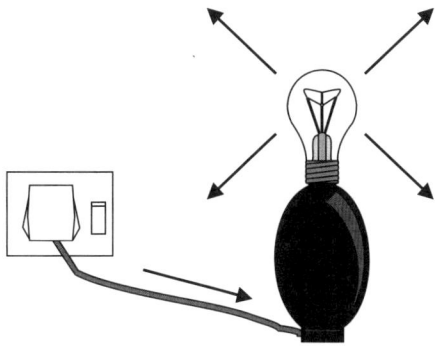

   (a) List three types of energy present in the diagram.

   ....

   (b) Complete the energy transfer for the lamp:

   .... energy → .... energy + ... energy

2. Energy transfers occur in many everyday situations.

   (a) For the each of following energy transfers, give a real life example.

   (i) kinetic → electrical

   ....

   (ii) light → electrical

   ....

   (iii) electrical → kinetic

   ....

   (iv) sound → electrical → sound

   ....

   (b) Name two types of stored energy.

   ....

   ....

Conservation of Energy & Efficiency of Machines

1. The diagram below is known as a Sankey diagram.
   This example shows how energy is transferred in a buzzer.

   (a) How much energy is wasted as heat?

   ....

   (b) What happens to this wasted energy?

   ....

   (c) How efficient is the buzzer?

   ....

2. In a traditional power station energy from fossil fuels is used to boil water.
   The high pressure steam produced is used to turn the turbines, which then generates electricity.

   The energy transfer diagram shows what happens to the energy.

   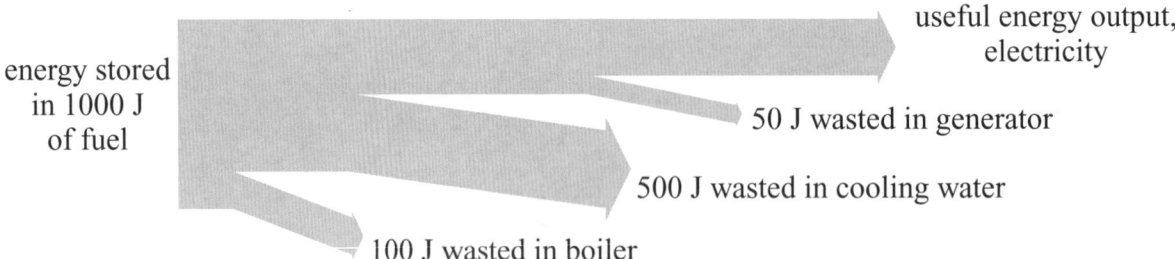

   (a) How much useful energy output is produced for every 1000 J of fuel?

   ....

   (b) 50% of the energy supplied by the fuel is wasted in cooling the water. Some power stations use this energy to heat local homes. This can increase the efficiency of the power station to 80%. Explain why this example of energy conservation is beneficial to the environment.

   ....

   ....

Section Five — Energy

Work Done, Energy and Power

1. A car travels at a constant speed for 1500 m. The force produced by the engine is 300 N.

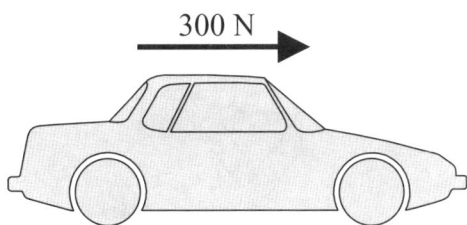

(a) What is the work done?

....

(b) It takes 5 minutes to complete the journey. Find the power output of the engine.

....

2. A crane's motor lifts a 40 kg mass into the air. Assume $g = 10$ m/s^2.

(a) Given that the work done is 40 000 Joules, how high is the mass lifted?

....

(b) It takes 7 minutes to lift the mass.
What is the power output of the motor? (Give your answer to 1 decimal place.)

....

3. A mechanic needs to buy a powerful motor.
He tests two motors and writes his results in the table below.

(a) Complete the table, giving the values for power to one decimal place.

motor	force (N)	distance (m)	work done (J)	time taken (s)	power (W)
A	300	50		180	
B	500	40		120	

(b) Which is the most powerful motor?

....

Section Five — Energy

Kinetic Energy and Potential Energy

1. A catapult is used to fire a stone that has a mass of 5 g.
   The stone travels at a velocity of 100 m/s.

   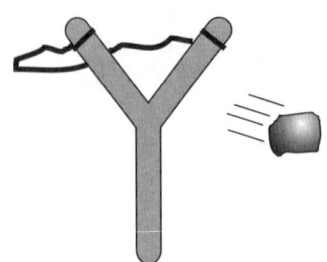

   (a) Calculate the kinetic energy of the stone.

   ....

   (b) A 5 g bullet is fired from a gun at a velocity of 1000 m/s.
   How many times the kinetic energy of the stone does the bullet have?

   ....

   ....

   (c) Use the results of (a) and (b) to explain why the speeding bullet can cause more damage.

   ....

   ....

2. Samantha is a bungee jumper.
   She jumps off a tall crane attached to a large elastic rope.

   (a) When will she have her maximum gravitational potential energy?

   ....

   (b) How much kinetic energy will she have at the bottom of her first bounce when the elastic rope is at full stretch?

   ....

   (c) When she bounces back, why does she not reach the height she started at?

   ....

Section Five — Energy

Kinetic Energy and Potential Energy

1. During the production of a new film, a dummy is dropped 60 m from the top of a building. The dummy's mass is 95 kg. Assume that g = 10 m/s².

    (a) How much potential energy does the dummy have before it is dropped?

    ....

    (b) How much kinetic energy will the dummy have when it reaches the ground? (Ignore the effect of air resistance.)

    ....

    (c) Calculate its speed as it hits the ground.

    ....

2. Tina skis down a hill.

    (a) Describe how her kinetic energy and potential energy change as she travels down the hill.

    ....

    ....

    (b) She uses an electric winch to get back to the top of the hill. It takes her 1 minute to reach the top, and she gains 3000 J of potential energy. What is the power output of the winch?

    ....

3. A child of mass 30 kg plays on a swing.

    ------- highest point of swing

    ------- lowest point of swing

    The difference between the highest and lowest points of the swing is 1.2 m.
    What is the child's fastest speed? Assume that g = 10 m/s², and show all your working.

    ....

    ....

Section Five — Energy

Heat Transfer

1. The diagram shows a cup designed to keep drinks hot. When the lid of the cup is closed, heat loss from the drink inside is greatly reduced.

   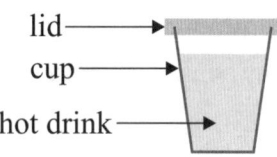

   (a) Suggest why the lid is so effective in reducing heat loss from the drink.

   ....

   ....

   (b) The cup is coloured white. Suggest how this also helps to keep the drink hot.

   ....

2. The diagram shows a type of immersion heater used in a hot water tank.

   (a) Explain why the top of the tank is the hottest.

   ....

   ....

   (b) Why is the tank lagged?

   ....

3. Heat inside a fridge is transferred to a coolant which passes through pipes on the back of the fridge.

   (a) Explain what colour these pipes should be painted.

   ....

   ....

   (b) How does placing the freezer compartment at the top of the fridge help to encourage convection currents in the main part of the fridge?

   ....

   ....

Conduction, Convection, and Radiation of Heat

1   Heat may be transferred by conduction, convection or radiation.

   (a) Using your ideas about thermal energy transfer, briefly explain why:

      (i) walking on carpet with bare feet feels warmer than walking on floor tiles.

      ....

      (ii) using two thin blankets on a bed is usually warmer than one thick one.

      ....

      (iii) astronauts wear suits made of a shiny material in space.

      ....

   (b) In winter, why is a cloud-free night colder than a cloudy night?

   ....

   ....

2   A physics student sets up an experiment as shown. The student records the temperature reading on both thermometers every two minutes.

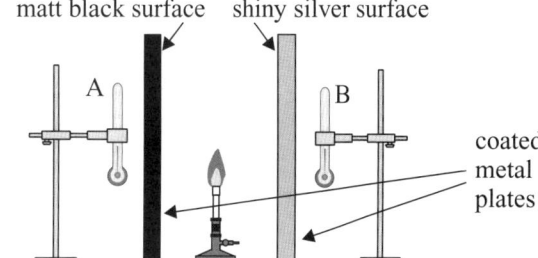

The graph shows the results for thermometer B.

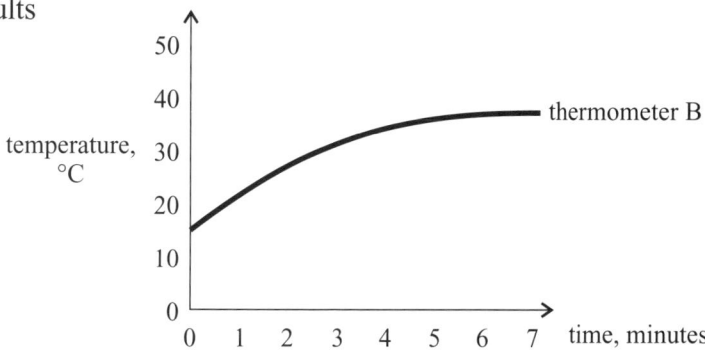

   (a) Draw the graph you would expect for thermometer A.

   (b) Explain the different shapes of the two graphs.

   ....

   ....

Section Five — Energy

Applications of Heat Transfer & Keeping Buildings Warm

1. A thermos flask is designed to keep drinks hot or cold.
   Thermal energy can be lost by conduction,
   convection or radiation.

   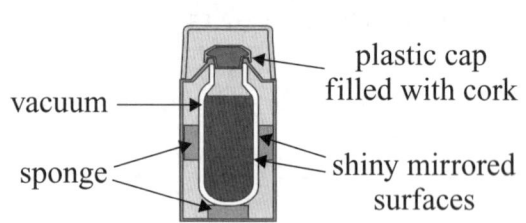

   Complete the table by ticking the columns which show
   the thermal energy transfer that each part of the flask prevents.

part of flask	type of thermal energy transfer prevented		
	conduction	convection	radiation
vacuum			
shiny mirrored surfaces			
sponge			
plastic cap filled with cork			

2. A typical house loses heat in several ways.

   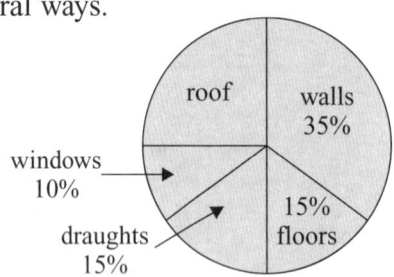

   (a) Why does heat energy leave the house?

   ....

   (b) Which part of the house most needs insulation?

   ....

   (c) What percentage of the heat lost is lost through the roof?

   ....

   (d) Suggest why the roof loses more thermal energy than the floors.

   ....

   (e) What could be done to reduce the thermal energy loss through the roof?

   ....

Section Five — Energy

Energy Resources

1. Explain where the following types of energy come from.

    (a) Nuclear power. ....

    ....

    (b) Geothermal energy. ....

    ....

    (c) Tidal energy. ....

    ....

2. A small community live on a remote island. They use coal and oil transported from the mainland as their main energy sources. The residents decide to put solar panels on their roofs and build some wind turbines to generate electricity.

    They now have four different energy sources: coal, oil, solar and wind.

    (a) Coal is a fossil fuel. Give one disadvantage for the islanders of using coal.

    ....

    (b) (i) Which two of the energy sources above are renewable?

    ....

    (ii) Explain clearly what is meant by a renewable energy source.

    ....

    (c) Suggest two reasons why the residents have chosen to use solar panels and wind turbines.

    ....

    ....

    (d) Give two factors that would be important in choosing a location for the wind turbines.

    ....

    ....

Section Five — Energy

Power Stations Using Non-Renewables

1. A coal-fired power station generates electricity for the National Grid.

   (a) Explain how energy from the coal is used to generate electricity.

   ....

   ....

   (b) Write down two environmental problems caused by burning coal to generate electricity.

   ....

   (c) Suggest two ways that these environmental problems could be reduced.

   ....

   ....

2. The table gives some information about the cost of energy resources.

source of energy	unit bought	cost per unit, £	thermal energy per unit, MJ	cost per MJ, p
natural gas	1 m³	0.12	40	0.30
oil	10 litres	2.00	370	0.54
coal	50 kg	7.50	1500	

   (a) Complete the table by calculating the cost per MJ for coal.

   (b) Using the information in the table, calculate the volume, in m³, of natural gas which would produce the same number of MJ of thermal energy as 1000 kg of coal.

   ....

3. Nuclear reactors can be used to generate electricity.

   (a) In what respect could nuclear power be described as "clean"?

   ....

   (b) The uranium fuel used in nuclear power stations is cheap.
   What factors cause the overall cost of nuclear power to be high?

   ....

   ....

Section Five — Energy

Wind Power and Hydroelectric Power

1   A small community of people live on an island. Each home used to have its own diesel generator to produce electricity. These were replaced by a combined wind and hydroelectric system to generate electricity for the whole island. During strong winds, the wind turbine alone provides enough electricity for the island.

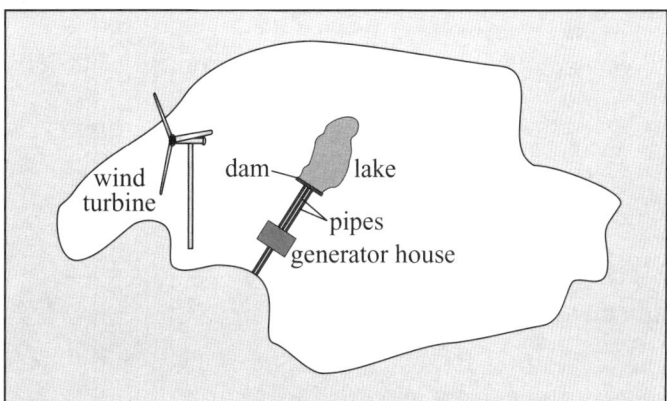

The island is usually fairly windy and has a small lake. The lake is used in the hydroelectric part of the system. The generator house contains a water turbine, which is used to generate electricity, and an electrically driven pump, which can be used to pump water from the river up into the lake.

(a) Explain when the water turbine would be used.

    ....

    ....

(b) Explain when the pump would be used.

    ....

    ....

(c) Write down two benefits to the environment of this scheme.

    ....

    ....

(d) Write down two environmental problems that may be caused by the hydroelectric system.

    ....

    ....

Section Five — Energy

Wave Power and Tidal Power

1. Waves form a potential worldwide energy resource.

   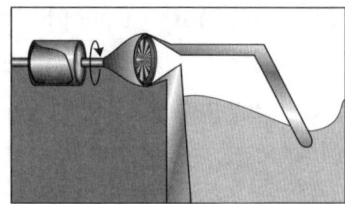

   (a) Explain how the wave movement is harnessed to produce electricity.

   ....

   ....

   (b) (i) Give two advantages of this system.

   ....

   (ii) Give two disadvantages of the system.

   ....

2. Tidal barrages are large dams built across river estuaries.

   (a) Explain how a tidal barrage can be used to generate electricity.

   ....

   ....

   (b) Are tidal barriers a reliable way of providing energy? Justify your answer.

   ....

   (c) Suggest two potential environmental problems with the use of tidal barrages for electricity production.

   ....

   ....

   (d) Explain how tidal barrages can be used to provide energy at times of peak demand.

   ....

   ....

Section Five — Energy

Geothermal and Wood Burning

1. The diagram shows electricity being generated using naturally occurring geological heat sources.

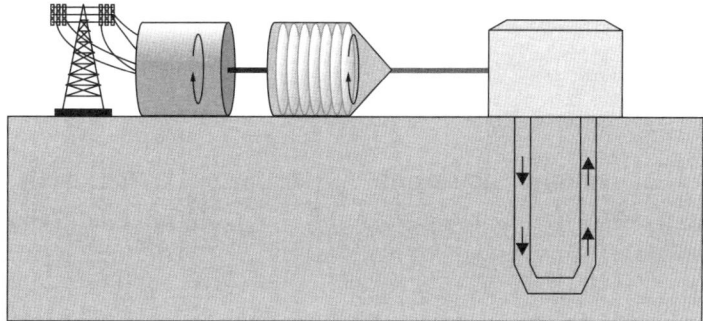

(a) Explain how this electricity is generated.

....

....

(b) What is the main expense involved in producing electricity in this way?

....

(c) Why are there only a few places in the world where this type of energy is an economic option?

....

2. In the future, the UK may make increasing use of wood burning in order to produce electricity. The wood used is sourced from specially cultivated forests. Wood burning in this way is economical, as well as having a low impact on the environment.

(a) Explain how burning wood can have a low impact on the environment.

....

....

(b) Is wood burning a renewable or non-renewable resource? Explain your answer.

....

....

Section Five — Energy

Solar Energy and Comparisons

1. Solar energy can be used in three different ways. One example is a solar cell which is a device that uses the photoelectric effect to generate electricity.

    (a) Name two devices that use solar cells as an energy source.

    ....

    (b) In many European countries houses have solar panels on their roofs to heat the household water. Fill in the missing labels to complete the diagram showing how a solar panel works.

    (c) Explain how electricity is produced by a solar furnace.

    ....

    ....

    (d) Give one example of a place where solar power would be essential.

    ....

2. There are many different methods of producing electricity.
   Complete the table by giving one advantage and one disadvantage of each method.

method of producing electricity	advantage	disadvantage
nuclear		
burning coal		
wind		
solar		

Section Five — Energy

Energy Mini-Exam (1)

1   During the 2002 Junior World Weightlifting Championships, division winner Yasen Stoyenov lifts a bar of mass 117.5 kg from the ground to a height of 2.15 m. For this question, assume g = 10 m/s².

(a) What type of energy has the bar gained?

....

(b) How much energy has the bar gained?

....

(c) (i) Use the formula "work done = force × distance" to calculate how much work the weightlifter did to lift the bar.

....

(ii) The lift took seven seconds. How much power did it take to lift the bar? Give your answer to 1 decimal place.

....

The weightlifter then drops the bar. As the bar falls an energy change takes place.

(d) Complete the energy change.

.... energy   →   .... energy

(e) If all the energy has been converted, what is the bar's speed as it hits the floor? (Give your answer to 2 decimal places.)

....

(f) What happens to the energy that was in the bar as it hits the floor?

....

Section Five — Energy

Energy Mini-Exam (2)

2   In the UK, it is important that houses should be insulated.

(a) What are the advantages of insulating a house?

....

(b) This pie chart shows the percentage heat losses from a house. Complete the diagram to show heat loss through the walls.

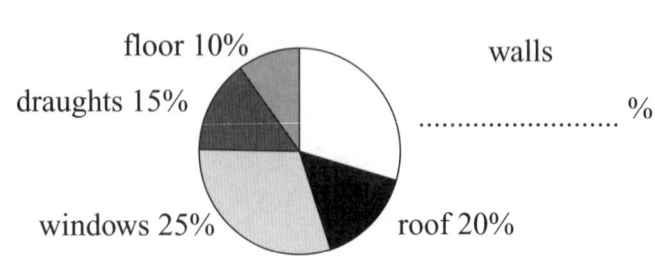

floor 10%
draughts 15%
walls ....%
windows 25%
roof 20%

(c) For each of the insulation methods below, explain how they reduce heat loss.

(i) Thick curtains. ....

....

(ii) Draught proofing. ....

....

3   Two double glazing salesmen claim that their company's double glazing will more than halve heat loss from the windows. Here are the details for the two companies' windows.

window type	heat lost by window, Joules per second	energy saved, Joules per second
ordinary single pane	235	0
Easy View double glazing	110	
NuGlars double glazing	119	

(a) Complete the table to show how much energy each company's windows save compared with single pane windows.

(b) Are the salesmen's claims true?

....

(c) How much energy is saved by NuGlars's windows each day?

....

Section Five — Energy

Energy Mini-Exam (3)

4   In many countries, nuclear power stations are used to produce electricity.
    The boxes show the main parts of a nuclear power station.

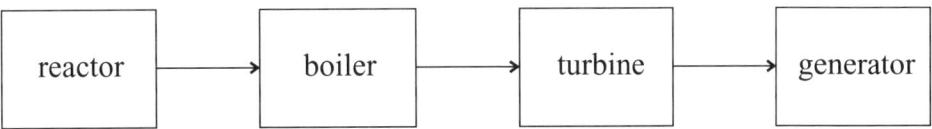

   (a) What useful energy transfer takes place in:

   (i) the reactor?

   ....

   (ii) the turbine?

   ....

   (iii) the generator?

   ....

   (b) Nuclear power stations produce waste.
       Explain the problems associated with the nuclear waste.

   ....

   ....

   (c) Describe three advantages of generating electricity using nuclear power,
       over other methods.

   ....

   ....

   ....

   (d) Explain whether nuclear power is a renewable or non-renewable resource.

   ....

   ....

Energy Mini-Exam (4)

5   Wood and coal are two fuels derived from plants.

(a) (i) What is the original source of the energy stored in wood and coal?

....

(ii) Explain why wood can be a renewable resource but coal is non-renewable.

....

....

(b) A modern power station grows its own fuel using fast-growing trees.
As the trees are cut down and burnt, more are planted to replace them.

carbon dioxide absorbed in photosynthesis   carbon dioxide and other waste gases

The company that owns the power station describes it as "non-polluting".

(i) Explain how the company could justify this statement.

....

....

(ii) Give another advantage of burning wood instead of coal in a power station.

....

....

(iii) Suggest why this method of generating electricity is not suitable for replacing all the power stations that burn fossil fuels.

....

....

Section Five — Energy

Section Six — Radioactivity

Atomic Structure and Isotopes

1. Copper has atomic number 29. It has two stable isotopes, copper-63 and copper-65. Write down brief answers to the questions below.

   (a) Which two types of nuclear particle are present in each nucleus of copper-63? Say how many there are of each type.

   Type 1: .... Number of this type in nucleus: ....

   Type 2: .... Number of this type in nucleus: ....

   (b) Why would a bar of copper-65 have more mass than a bar of copper-63 of the same size?

   ....

   ....

   (c) A pure sample of copper-64, an unstable isotope of copper, is left for an hour in a sealed container. Explain why when the container is opened small amounts of other elements are found with the copper.

   ....

   ....

2. Ernest Rutherford carried out a famous experiment in which a beam of alpha particles was fired at gold foil. The diagram below shows a close-up of four of the atoms in a sheet of gold foil.

   (a) Complete the diagram to show what would happen to each of the alpha particles being fired at the gold foil. The first one has been done for you.

   (diagram not to scale)

   (b) Explain how this experiment disproved the "plum pudding" model of the atom.

   ....

   ....

The Three Types of Radiation

1. The following statements concern alpha, beta and gamma radiation.
   For each statement, explain whether it is true or false.

   (a) Radiation can't hurt you because you can't see it.

   ....

   ....

   (b) A thick pair of shoes would protect you against radiation coming from a floor contaminated by an alpha emitter.

   ....

   ....

   (c) Polythene gloves would protect you from a beta emitter.

   ....

   (d) A lead suit (2 mm thick) would protect you against gamma radiation.

   ....

   ....

   (e) Gamma rays are electrically charged, unlike alpha particles.

   ....

   ....

2. A radiation leak produces alpha, beta and gamma radiation that passes into a man's leg.

   (a) Which of the three types of radiation will pass through his leg and emerge on the other side?

   ....

   (b) Which type of radiation is likely to cause most ionisation in the man's leg?
   Explain your answer.

   ....

   ....

Section Six — Radioactivity

Background Radiation

1. An atom of the radioactive isotope Thorium-234 has just been created by radioactive decay. The half life of Thorium-234 is 24 days. Which of the statements below is definitely true?

    A: That particular atom will decay after 24 days.

    B: That particular atom will decay after 48 days.

    C: You cannot tell when that particular atom will decay.

    D: The atom will last forever.

    ....

2. Background radiation is different in different places, and at different times.

    (a) Janine wants to measure the amount of radiation coming from a radiation source. Explain why she must first measure the amount of radiation in the room with the source still shielded.

    ....

    ....

    (b) Explain why people living in certain areas of the UK can expect to be exposed to higher levels of radiation than people living elsewhere.

    ....

    ....

    (c) As an aeroplane climbs into the sky, how would the amount of radiation detected inside the plane change? Explain your answer.

    ....

    ....

3. The pie chart below shows the sources of background radiation. Write in the labels "medical X-rays", "the nuclear industry" and "radon and thoron gas" on the correct segments of the pie.

Section Six — Radioactivity

Uses of Radioactive Materials

1. There are two forms of the element Technetium-99. Ordinary Technetium-99 has a half-life of 212 000 years. Another form called Technetium-99m has a half-life of six hours.

    (a) Which form is suitable for injecting into a patient to check the health of their heart? Explain your answer.

    ....

    ....

    (b) Why is a radioactive tracer that gives off gamma rays less of a health risk than a tracer that gives off beta particles?

    ....

    ....

    (c) Complete this sentence: "It is impossible to use substances that emit alpha particles as tracers within the human body because alpha radiation cannot

    ...."

2. There are many varied uses for radioactive sources.

    (a) For some of its length a river runs underground. Write a paragraph on how a radioactive isotope could be used to find out the route the water takes under the ground. Explain what sort of radiation source would be most suitable.

    ....

    ....

    ....

    (b) Which of these radiation sources would be the best to use for sterilising surgical instruments?

source	type of radiation	half-life
radon-222	alpha	3.8 days
technetium-99m	gamma	6 hours
americium-241	alpha	458 years
cobalt-60	gamma	5.26 years

    ....

Section Six — Radioactivity

Uses of Radioactive Materials

1   The thickness of plastic film can be controlled during its manufacture using a radioactive source. The film is passed through rollers, then between the source and a detector. The amount of radiation detected is used to control the separation of the rollers.
    The diagram below shows the machinery used.

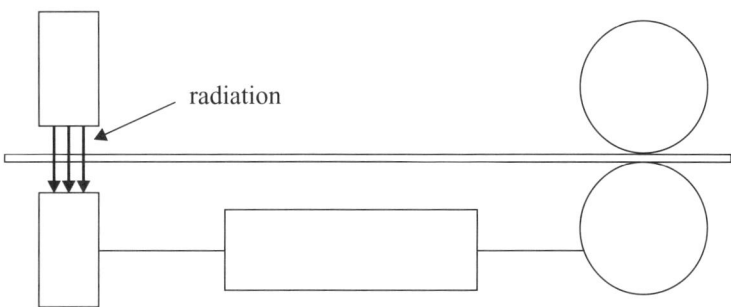

   (a) Label the **plastic film**, **rollers**, **radiation source**, **radiation detector** and the **control unit** for the rollers.

   (b) Should alpha, beta or gamma radiation be used? Give a reason for your choice.

   ....

   ....

   (c) The radiation recorded by the detector goes up.
       What does this tell you about the thickness of the film?

   ....

   (d) What is a sensible choice of half-life for the source? Explain your answer.

   ....

   ....

2   The following statements 1, 2 and 3 are about radioactive dating of igneous rocks.
    Tick one box to show which of the statements are true.

       Statement 1: When igneous rocks are formed they contain uranium.
       Statement 2: Uranium decays to lead.
       Statement 3: The higher the proportion of uranium in the rock, the older the rock is.

    ☐ 1, 2 and 3   ☐ 1 and 2   ☐ 2 and 3   ☐ 1 and 3

Section Six — Radioactivity

Detection of Radiation

1. A scientist wants to measure the amount of radiation emitted by a radioactive source.

   (a) What piece of equipment could she use to do this?

   ....

   (b) The scientist places this piece of equipment close to the source and records her measurement. Explain why this result is not equal to the amount of radiation emitted by the source.

   ....

   ....

2. A Geiger-Müller tube placed near a radiation source registers 87 decays in 30 seconds.

   (a) A different Geiger-Müller tube placed at an equal distance from the same radioactive source over the same time period gives a larger reading in Becquerels. Suggest why.

   ....

   ....

   ....

   (b) If the results from the two Geiger-Müller tubes are used to calculate the half-life of the source, will the two calculations give the same result? Explain your answer.

   ....

   ....

3. When Alan goes to the dentist he notices that the dental technician who X-rays his teeth wears a badge containing photographic film.

   (a) What happens to the film in normal use?

   ....

   (b) Why does the badge have a date written on it?

   ....

   ....

Section Six — Radioactivity

Radiation Hazards and Safety

1. Sources of alpha radiation are handled in a nuclear plant in "glove boxes". These are made from thin aluminium with a perspex window that the worker can look through while he handles the source wearing thick rubber gloves.

    (a) Why is thicker shielding than thin aluminium not needed?

    ....

    ....

    (b) The boxes are kept at a pressure lower than atmospheric pressure.
    Why is this important in case of a leak such as a split in the rubber glove?

    ....

    ....

    (c) Why would breathing in an alpha emitter be hazardous to the worker?

    ....

    ....

2. After the explosion and fire at the Chernobyl nuclear power plant in 1986, many people in the area died of radiation sickness and cancer.

    (a) Describe how ionising radiation striking living cells causes:

    (i) radiation sickness; ....

    ....

    (ii) cancer. ....

    ....

    (b) Many of the firefighters who rushed to put out the fire died within days.
    Were they killed by radiation sickness or cancer?

    ....

Section Six — Radioactivity

Nuclear Equations and Half-Life

1. A series of radioactive decays will eventually cause a nucleus of uranium-238 to become lead-206. This chart of atomic number against mass number shows the first steps of the series.

    The decay starts at the top right. Nucleus A is $^{238}_{92}U$.

name of element	atomic number	\multicolumn{9}{c}{mass number}
		230	231	232	233	234	235	236	237	238
uranium (U)	92									A
protactinium (Pr)	91					decay 2	C		decay 1	
thorium (Th)	90						B			
actinium (A)	89									

    (a) (i) What is meant by "mass number" and "atomic number"?

    ....

    ....

    (ii) In Decay 1 the nucleus of $^{238}_{92}U$ throws off an alpha particle and turns into a thorium nucleus, shown as "B" in the diagram. What is the mass number and atomic number of the thorium nucleus?

    ....

    (b) Write down the nuclear equation for Decay 1.

    ....

    (c) Write down the nuclear equation for Decay 2.

    ....

    (d) In Decay 3, Nucleus C decays to Nucleus D by emitting a beta particle, then that nucleus emits an alpha particle to become Nucleus E. On the chart, sketch in two arrows representing the two decays and show where Nucleus D and Nucleus E would appear.

2. A radioactive sample of francium shows a radioactivity of 320 Becquerels. After 1 hour 45 minutes this has dropped to 10 Bq. What is its half-life? Show your working.

    ....

    ....

Section Six — Radioactivity

Half-Life Calculations

1. When a sample of igneous rock was formed it contained some uranium-238.
The diagrams below show graphically the proportion of uranium (chemical symbol U) atoms that have decayed to lead (chemical symbol Pb) after various times. Diagram 1 shows the situation when the rock was formed and Diagram 3 the situation after 8.94 billion years.

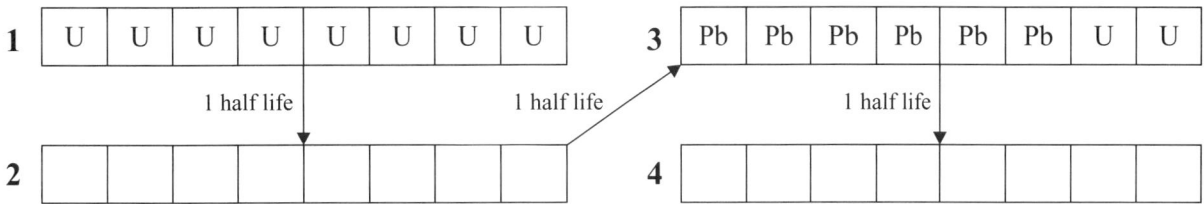

(a) In diagram 2, show the proportion of atoms that have decayed after 4.47 billion years.

(b) In diagram 4, show the proportion of atoms that have decayed after 13.41 billion years.

(c) What is the half-life of uranium-238? Tick the correct answer.

☐ 8.94 billion years   ☐ 4.47 billion years

☐ 13.41 billion years   ☐ 17.88 billion years

2. The count rate near a sample of radioactive copper-64 was measured with a Geiger counter over several days. The graph below shows the results.

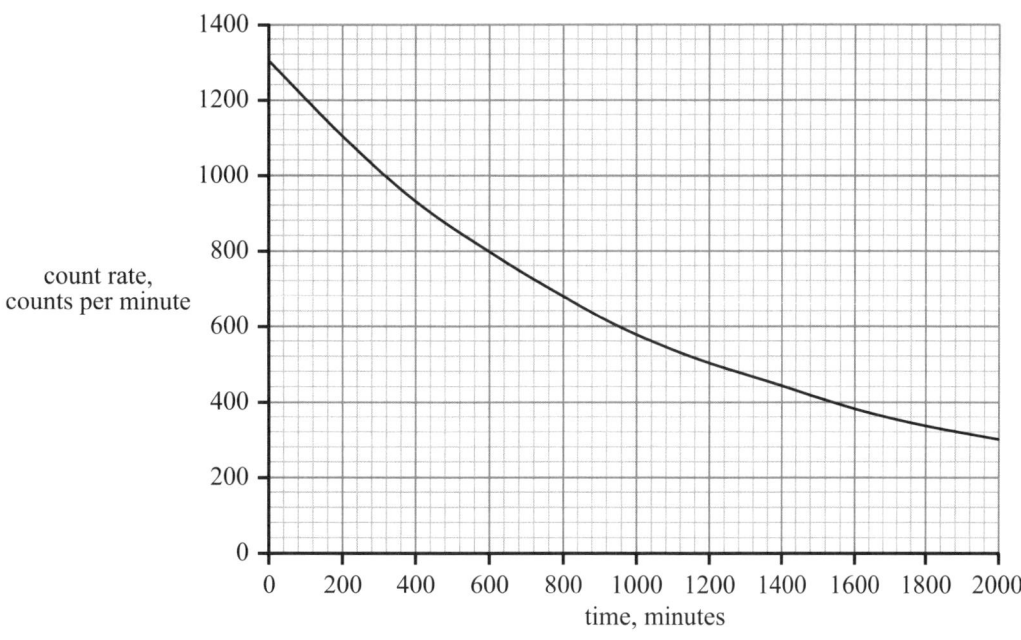

Before the copper-64 was brought out of storage, the background count rate in the laboratory had been a steady 100 counts per minute. Find the half-life of copper-64.

....

Section Six — Radioactivity

Radioactivity Mini-Exam (1)

1. An atom of the radioactive isotope uranium-238 is made up of electrons, protons and neutrons.

    (a) Write down "electron", "proton" and "neutron" in the correct places in the table below.

		electric charge		
		-1	0	+1
mass	1/2000			
	1			

    (b) Explain the meanings of both words in the phrase "radioactive isotope".

    ....

    ....

    (c) State three practical uses for radioactive materials.

    ....

    ....

2. Samples of igneous rock containing potassium-40 (half-life 1.26 billion years) are often also found to contain trapped argon gas.

    (a) (i) Where did this gas come from?

    ....

    (ii) How can the gas be used to date the rock?

    ....

    ....

    ....

    (b) In one rock sample the ratio of potassium-40 to argon-40 was found to be 1:15. How old is it?

    ....

    ....

Section Six — Radioactivity

Radioactivity Mini-Exam (2)

3   The diagram below explains how a smoke alarm works.

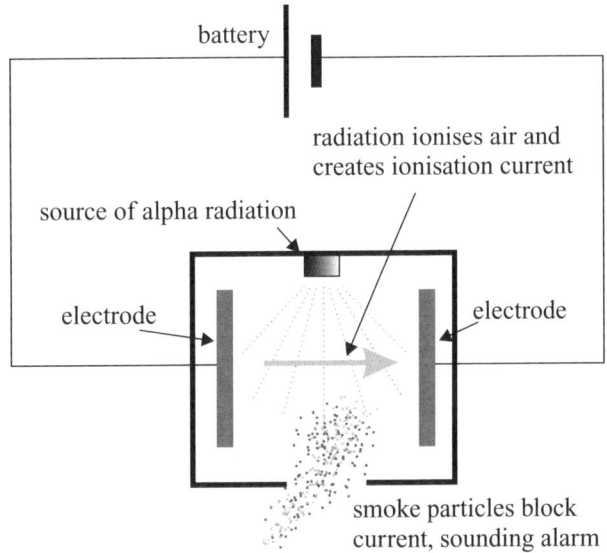

(a) Describe what happens to an individual atom when it is ionised by radiation.

   ....

   ....

(b) Both a smoke detector and a Geiger-Müller tube rely on the fact that a current can flow through an ionised gas. Choose from the phrases below to complete this table comparing the two devices.

   current flows around circuit   no current flows around circuit   inside   outside

	What happens to the ionisation current while nothing is being detected?	What happens to the current when the machine detects something?	Is the radioactive source inside or outside the chamber?
smoke alarm			
Geiger-Müller tube			

(c) Explain why using a Geiger-Müller tube to detect gamma radiation tends to be a long slow job compared to using it to detect alpha and beta radiation.

   ....

   ....

Section Six — Radioactivity

Radioactivity Mini-Exam (3)

4   Approximately one in ten million carbon molecules found in living plants or animals are the radioactive isotope carbon-14, absorbed from the air. After a plant or animal dies this proportion starts to decrease. Carbon-14 has a half-life of 5700 years.

   (a) Calculate the fraction of the atoms in a pure sample of carbon-14 that will still not have decayed after ten half-lives have gone by.

   ....

   ....

   (b) Approximately how old is a bone fragment in which the proportion of carbon-14 is one part in fifty million? Explain your answer.

   ....

   ....

   ....

   (c) Suggest why carbon dating is unreliable for samples more than around 50 000 to 60 000 years old.

   ....

   ....

5   The diagram shows the radioactive decay of an atom.

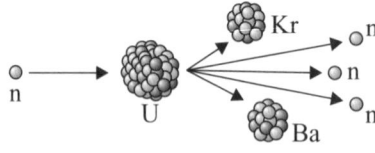

   (a) What is the name of the type of radioactive decay shown in the diagram?

   ....

   (b) Describe the process of radioactive decay shown in the diagram.

   ....

   ....

Section Six — Radioactivity

Let's face it, you want CGP Revision Books — not other people's dreary stuff.

Everyone else just gives you dreary revision books with only the boring stuff in and no entertainment. Boo. Hiss.
We're different — we always try and make sure you're gonna enjoy using our books.

What you *really* need is a **Free Catalogue** showing the full range of CGP Revision Books.
That way you can be sure you're not missing out on a brilliant book that **might just save your life**.

Order your Free Catalogue today
— and you'll probably have it by tomorrow

 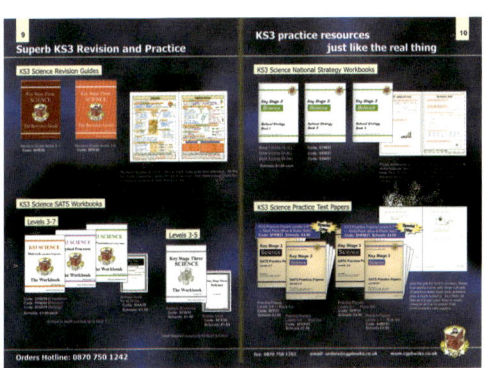

FIVE ways to get your Free Catalogue really quickly:

1) Orders Hotline: 0870 750 1252
   You can ring our cheerful, friendly operators Mon-Fri, 8.30am to 5.30pm.

2) The CGP website
   You can order anytime at: **www.cgpbooks.co.uk**

3) E-mail
   You can simply **e-mail** your order: **orders@cgpbooks.co.uk**

4) FAX
   You can use the good old **FAX** machine: **0870 750 1292**

5) Post
   Finally there's snail mail (we recommend you use a First Class stamp):

   CGP, Kirkby in Furness, Cumbria, LA17 7WZ

0704 - 1776

Do not chew.

ISBN 1 84146 225 X

PHQ41

Coordination Group Publications

www.cgpbooks.co.uk

Visit the CGP website for the
full picture of our entire range

GCSE
Physics
Essential Exam Practice

Higher Level

CGP					Answers

Section One — Electricity and Magnetism

Page 1
1 (a) Electrons, negative charge / -1 charge.
  (b) The current increases.
  (c) The sodium chloride solution contains ions / charged particles that are free to move. Their movement creates an electric current.
2 The higher the resistance, the lower the current.
3 (a) DC keeps flowing in the same direction all the time.
     AC keeps reversing its direction, back and forth.
  (b)

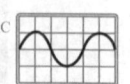 

Your diagrams don't have to be identical to these, but the key features must be there. AC is a wave, and DC is a flat horizontal line.

Page 2
1 (a)

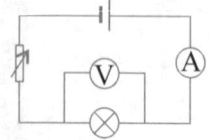

As always, the ammeter must be connected in series, and the voltmeter connected in parallel.

  (b)

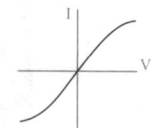

  (c) R = V ÷ I = 12 ÷ 1.6
       = 7.5 Ω
2 (a) (i)

     (ii)

  (b) 120 mA = 0.120 A
     Use V = IR:
     Initial p.d. = 0.120 × 40 = 4.8 V
     Final p.d. = 0.120 × 50 = 6.0 V
     Change in p.d. = 6.0 − 4.8 = 1.2 V
3 Diode or semiconductor diode. It allows current to flow in one direction only (shown by the way the symbol is pointing).

Page 3
1 (a) If connected in parallel the motor would always have the full supply voltage across it. Having them in series allows you to control the amount of current through the motor and so the speed of the car.
  (b) 12 − 5.5 = 6.5 V
  (c) B
2 (a) 10 + 5 + 5 = 20 Ω
  (b) (i) I = V ÷ R
         = 4 ÷ 10
         = 0.4 A (current through 10 Ω resistor is the same as current in all parts of the circuit)
     (ii) V = IR
         = 0.4 × 20
         = 8 V

Make sure you show all your working. That way, even if you mess up somewhere, you still get method marks. It makes it easier for you to check your answers as well.

Page 4
1 (a) Any two from:
     Lights can be switched on/off independently.
     Failure of one bulb leaves the others unaffected.
     Each bulb runs from the full 230 V mains supply.
  (b) $A_2 = A_1 + A_3$
2 (a) (i) 4 × 0.5 = 2.0 A
     (ii) 0 A
     (iii) (4 × 0.5) + (2 × 6.0) = 14.0 A

Remember to give the units. If you miss them off, your answer could be in amps or volts or horsepower. Even when you think it's obvious what the units are, the examiners still want to see 'em.

  (b) The battery (or alternator) can't provide the full voltage when there is a high current / heavy load.

Page 5
1 (a) Electrons move from rod to cloth.
  (b) Electrons in the tissue paper are attracted towards the positively charged rod, giving the part of the paper closest to the rod a negative charge (which attracts the paper to the rod), and the part furthest from the rod a positive charge. The attraction is stronger than the repulsion because the negative charge is closer to the rod than the positive charge.
  (c) (i) Distance *d* must be large enough to prevent a spark jumping across the gap from the cables to earth.
     (ii) The higher the voltage, the larger distance *d* will need to be to prevent a spark.

Page 6
1 (a) Plate A would be negative and Plate B would be positive.
  (b) By adjusting the size and the polarity (direction) of the voltage applied to the plates, the amount the ink droplets move up or down can be precisely controlled.
  (c) Droplets of different mass would be affected differently by the electrical force / would accelerate at different rates / would be deflected by different amounts / would reduce print quality.
2 (a) Electrons are attracted from earth through the person to the car to neutralize the positive charge on the car.
  (b) (i) Fuel flowing out of the filler pipe can cause an electrostatic charge to build up. This can cause a spark and ignite the fuel.
     (ii) Use an earthing strap between the filler pipe and the fuel tank.
         OR Use a metal filler pipe so that charge is conducted safely away.

Page 7
1 LED: electrical to light
   Cell: chemical to electrical
   Motor: electrical to kinetic
2 Wire A has a lower resistance than wire B. The lower the resistance, the greater the current flowing through the wire, therefore the more heat is produced.

If you find this hard to understand, just learn it off by heart:
      more resistance = less current = less heating

3 (a) E = QV
       = 10 × 3
       = 30 J

Remember — always show your working, and always give the units.

  (b) (i) V = E / Q for the resistor
         = 8 ÷ 10
         = 0.8 V
     (ii) p.d. across motor = 3.0 − 0.8 = 2.2 V
         E = QV
         = 10 × 2.2
         = 22 J
         OR
         Energy supplied by the battery = QV = 10 × 3
                                              = 30 J as before.
         Energy to motor = 30 − 8 = 22 J

Page 8
1. A
2. (a) kilowatt-hour or kWh

    NOT kilowatt per hour, that's Wrong Wrong Wrong. (Remember, a kilowatt-hour is the amount of electrical energy used by a 1kW appliance left on for 1 hour.)

   (b) 1 kWh = 1000 W × 3600 s

      = 3 600 000 J

      = 3.6 MJ

      500 units = 500 × 3.6

      = 1800 MJ

   (c) 100 W = 0.1 kW

      Units used = 0.1 × 6

      = 0.6 kWh

      Cost = units × price = 0.6 × 8

      = 4.8 p

   (d) Cost of units = 500 × 8

      = 4000 p

      = £40.00

      Total cost = £40.00 + £8.50

      = £48.50

      Forgot the £8.50 standing charge? You need to read the question more carefully pal. Harsh but fair. You don't want to throw marks away by missing easy bits out.

3. (a) 90 min = 1.5 h

      3 kW × 1.5 h = 4.5 kWh = 4.5 units

   (b) Sam pays 50 ÷ 4.5 = 11.1 p per unit

      Landlord's profit = 11.1 – 10 = 1.1 p per unit.

Page 9
1. (a) ... live ... neutral ... yellow and green ... live ... metal ...

   (b) 230 V

2. (a) A large current flows through the live wire, passes through the metal case and out down the earth wire. The large current causes the fuse to melt and cuts off the live supply.

   (b) (i) live and neutral

      (ii) It doesn't need an earth wire because the case is made of plastic and there are no metal parts showing.

Page 10
1. (a) power = current × voltage or P = IV

      I = P/V

      = 300 ÷ 230 = 1.30 A

   (b) 3 A

   (c) The fuse should be rated a little higher than the normal current — next value above 1.3 A is 3 A.

2. (a) Transformers

   (b) Transformer 1 is a step-up transformer / it increases the voltage.

      Transformer 2 is a step-down transformer / it reduces the voltage.

   (c) The transformers.

   (d) P = IV

      I = P/V

      = 1 000 000 ÷ 25 000 = 40 A

   (e) P = IV

      I = P/V

      = 1 000 000 ÷ 400 000 = 2.5 A

      Hard to believe that pylon cables have such a tiny current. Less than a kettle. But they do — because the voltage is so high.

   (f) The greater the current, the greater the amount of energy lost as heat. Using a very high voltage means that the current can be kept very low, reducing heat loss in the cables.

Page 11
1. (a) and (b)

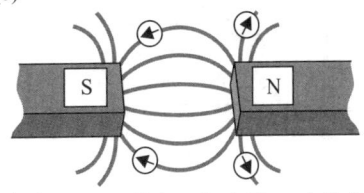

   The only thing you need to know to do this one is that the direction of the magnetic field is always from North to South.

   (c) A magnetic <u>field</u> is a region where a magnetic material, such as <u>iron</u> or <u>steel</u> (or nickel) experiences a <u>force</u>.

   (d) Both have the same shape magnetic field. / Both have opposite poles at the ends.

   (e) Circular field lines drawn, clockwise direction. For example:

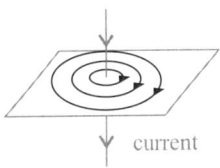

2. He is facing SOUTH, because the magnetic poles are opposite to the geographic poles (the south pole of the bar magnet is attracted to a north magnetic pole which is at the Earth's geographic south pole).

Page 12
1. (a) End X is a north pole. End Y is a south pole.

      This is a standard question — which pole is which on a solenoid. Where the current goes clockwise, that's the south pole. Anticlockwise? That'll be the north pole then.

   (b) repel

   (c) Solenoid A has a weaker magnetic field / Solenoid B has a stronger field / The magnetic fields are in opposite directions (as diagrams are shown).

   (d) Increase the current in solenoid A (double it), and reverse the current.

2. (a) No

   (b) She used iron instead of steel. She used AC instead of DC.

Page 13
1. (a) ... soft ... iron ... increases ...

   (b) steel nail, nickel-plated spoon

2.

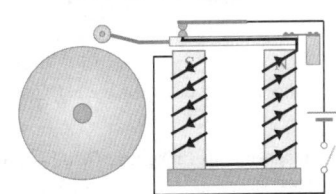

   The slope / shape of the coils drawn isn't important, as long as the arrows point from <u>right to left</u> on the left magnet and <u>left to right</u> on the right one. Where the current goes clockwise, that's the south pole. Anticlockwise? That'll be the north pole then.

3. (a) In the live wire.

   (b) If the electric current is too high, the electromagnet creates a strong enough field to pull down an iron rocker and break the circuit, i.e. it performs the same functions as a fuse. It can be pushed back into position (i.e. reset) once the current drops to its usual value.

Page 14
1. (a) The coil at the centre would become an electromagnet.

   (b) The paper cone would move either in or out.

   (c) You would hear nothing. The coil is attached to DC and not AC and does not vibrate back and forth. As the cone is not vibrating, it will not produce any sound.

2 (a) to (d)

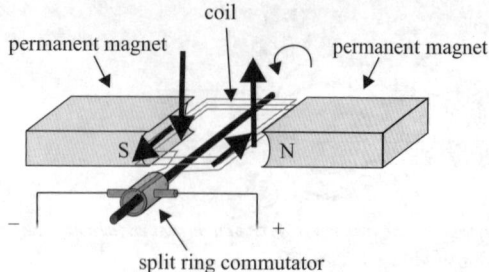

If you found this hard, that's because it is. Parts (a) and (b) are OK, but for (c) you need to use Fleming's Left Hand Rule. Pick one side of the coil. The f̲ield (first finger) goes from north to south, the m̲otion (thumb) goes as per the rotation arrow, giving you the c̲urrent (second finger). What a palaver.

(e) Any two of:
Increase the electric current / increase the number of turns on the coil / use a stronger magnet / wind the coil on a soft iron core.

Page 15

1 (a) AC voltage is induced, because the coil experiences a changing magnetic field.
(b) None, though the voltage would be in the opposite direction.
(c) It is an AC voltage.
(d) The CRO will show twice as many waves / peaks, and they will be higher / greater amplitude.

2 (a) How quickly the conductor/wire/coil passes through the magnetic field lines.
(b) C 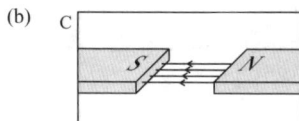   D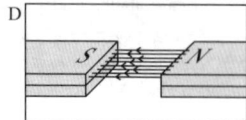

Page 16

1 (a) (i) The transformer is a step-down transformer.
No marks for "Decepticon".
(ii) Step-up transformer.
No marks for "Autobot".
(b) (i) 1000
(ii) 50
(c) number of turns on primary ÷ number of turns on secondary
= 1000 ÷ 50
= 20:1
(d) The output voltage is 0 (zero) V, because the input voltage is DC.
(e) (i) Iron.
(ii) The iron core transfers the magnetic flux / magnetic field from the primary coil to the secondary coil.
(iii) It would heat up (due to eddy currents flowing in the solid iron) and waste energy.

Page 17

1 (a) (i)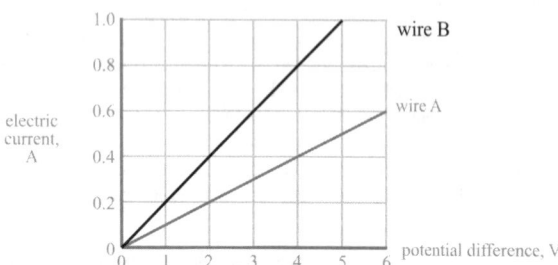
(ii) The current would have been too big for the 1 A ammeter.
(iii) Wire A has a 10 Ω resistance, wire B has a 5 Ω resistance.
OR wire A has twice the resistance of wire B.
OR wire A has a greater resistance than wire B.

(iv) Voltmeter in correct place in parallel with wire, ammeter anywhere in series. For example:

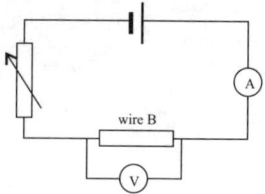

(b) A filament lamp will give a graph which is a curve. The resistance of the filament increases / current increases less quickly as voltage is increased because it gets hotter.

Page 18

2 (a) (i) Electrons / negative charges move from the duster to the polythene rod.
(ii) It becomes positive.
(iii) Positive.
(b) Two insulating materials are rubbed together, which causes electrons to move from one material to the other. Ann's slippers either have too many electrons (they're negatively charged) or too few (positively charged). When she touches the earthed radiator, electrons either move from earth through her to the slippers producing a shock, or from her slippers to the earth producing a shock.

3 (a) (i) The gas is burned to heat water in the boiler to make steam, which turns a turbine. This is connected to a generator, which consists of an electromagnet inside coils of wire. The generator produces electricity by induction.

*With these "explain" questions, go into as much detail as you can, within the space you've been given.
Make sure you keep it relevant though — don't mention the transformer, because it's not involved in generating the electricity.*

Page 19

(ii) Using a very high voltage means that the current can be kept very low, reducing heat loss in the cables. (The greater the current, the greater the amount of energy lost as heat.)
(b) To increase the voltage from 2 V to 12 V, the transformer must have a turns ratio of 1:6. Therefore, the secondary coil must have 120 turns.

4 (a) R = V / I
= 6 ÷ 0.25
= 24 Ω
(b) The potential difference / voltage stays the same but the resistance in the circuit increases / is doubled. The current is therefore less / halved and both bulbs glow dimly / less brightly than before.
(c) Put both bulbs in parallel with the power supply.

That's because when they're connected in parallel, they'll both get the full 6 V from the power supply.

Page 20

5 (a) P = IV so I = P/V
= 2760 ÷ 240
= 11.5 A
(b) He has caused the main fuse to melt, because he is taking 2 × 11.5 = 23 A for the heaters and has added 9 A for the kettle, giving a total of 32 A through a 30 A fuse.
(c) (i) live
(ii) The earth wire protects the user from electric shock — if there is a fault on the live wire and it touches the metal case, a big current flows to earth causing the fuse to melt.
(d) 1 kW × 0.5 h = 0.5 kWh per day
7 × 0.5 = 3.5 kWh per week
3.5 kWh × 6 p = 21 p

© 2004 CGP

Section Two — Forces and Motion

Page 21
1 (a) Mass represents the amount of matter in his body. It's the same anywhere. Weight is the pull of gravity on this mass. It depends on the gravitational field strength.

This is usually the best way to tackle "Explain the difference between..." questions — explain what each of the things is. It's crucial to understand the difference between weight and mass. Don't mix them up.

  (b) W = m × g
  = 90 × 10
  = 900 N

  (c) (i) Moment = force × distance to pivot
  = 900 × 1.5
  = 1350 Nm

  (ii) anticlockwise moment = clockwise moment
  1350 = slab force × 0.5
  slab force = 1350 ÷ 0.5
  = 2700 N

2 The weight of the astronauts is less on the Moon / gravity is less on the Moon. Therefore a flimsy ladder can support this smaller weight.

Page 22
1 (a) Reaction force.

  (b) Downward arrow labelled weight.

  (c) (i) Drag / air resistance.

   (ii) The new shape is more streamlined than the old shape.

   (iii) Top speed is reached when drag equals the driving force from the engine. For the streamlined shape, this amount of drag will occur at a higher speed than it does for the less streamlined shape.

  (d) Many possible answers. For example: Between the tyres and the road / in the braking system (i.e. between brake calipers and discs) / holding nuts and bolts together.

Page 23
1 (a) If object A exerts a force on object B then object B exerts an equal and opposite force on object A.

  (b) The skateboard exerts a force on Karl to move him (to the left on the diagram), so Karl exerts a force on the skateboard to move it (to the right on the diagram).

  (c) Objects moving at a steady speed have no resultant force. An unbalanced force (friction) is actually slowing the skateboard down.

2 (a) Paul's, because it will have the lowest overall mass.

This is down to the old favourite, Acceleration = Force ÷ Mass. So, if the force is the same, the one with the least mass will have the greatest acceleration. Which is why racing cars don't weigh much.

  (b) acceleration = force ÷ mass
  = 200 ÷ 90
  = 2.22 m/s^2

  (c) force = mass × acceleration
  = 90 × 5
  = 450 N

Page 24
1 (a) speed = distance ÷ time
  = 200 ÷ 16
  = 12.5 m/s

  (b) time = distance ÷ speed
  = 200 ÷ 11.9
  = 16.8 s

2 (a) Velocity depends on direction as well as speed. If the two planes are travelling in different directions their velocities are different.

  (b) Each plane needs to travel 280 m (half of 560 m).
  time = distance ÷ speed
  = 280 ÷ 140
  = 2 s

  (c) change in velocity = acceleration × time
  = 20 × 2
  = 40 m/s
  new velocity = 140 – 40
  = 100 m/s

  (d) Acceleration = change in velocity ÷ time
  = 120 ÷ 7.5
  = 16 m/s^2

Page 25
1 (a) velocity = distance ÷ time
  = 30 ÷ 0.1
  = 300 m/s

  (b) Find the deceleration by working out the gradient of the velocity time graph (ignoring the minus sign which means it's decelerating, not accelerating).
  Gradient = 300 ÷ (0.10 – 0.11) = 300 ÷ –0.01 = –30 000 m/s^2
  So deceleration is 30 000 m/s^2

...Aye, 'tis true, gradient of a velocity-time graph = acceleration. That's because the gradient is "vertical ÷ horizontal", i.e. "change in velocity ÷ time". Ain't science grand?

  (c) Distance travelled is area under graph.
  = 0.5 × 300 × 0.01
  = 1.5 m

2 (a) From 60 s to 120 s.

  (b) Both lines are straight (initially).

  (c) Train 1 is fastest.
  Speed = gradient
  = 60 ÷ 40
  = 1.5 cm/s

  (d) From 40 s to 80 s.

Page 26
1 (a) 10 000 + 40 000 = 50 000 N

  (b) acceleration = force ÷ mass
  = 50 000 ÷ 2000
  = 25 m/s^2

2 (a) Weight / Gravity

  (b) 700 N

Confused? The clue's in the question — "at a steady speed". That means the weight and drag forces must be balanced. Weight = 700 N, so drag = 700 N.

  (c) She now has a resultant force upwards. This accelerates her upwards, reducing her downward velocity.

  (d) 700 N

Page 27
1 (a) The distance the car travels in the split-second between a hazard appearing and the driver applying the brakes.

  (b) Visibility, Tiredness of driver

If you get close to the speed of light, time itself starts to get distorted. The universe around you seems to speed up. I guess that would increase your thinking distance too. My advice is stick below, say, 10 000 000 mph.

  (c) None. Ice would affect braking distance, not thinking distance.

2 (a) distance travelled = speed × time
  so travelling at a higher speed for the same amount of time increases the distance.

  (b) stopping distance = braking distance + thinking distance
  = 32 + 12
  = 44 m

  (c) In order to stop, the kinetic energy (½mv^2) has to be transformed into heat energy at the brakes and tyres:
  kinetic energy transferred = work done by brakes
  ½mv^2 = f × d
  (where d is the braking distance, and f is the maximum possible braking force, which is a constant and doesn't depend on speed)
  If the speed v doubles, then d must increase by a factor of four to make the equation balance.

© 2004 CGP

Page 28
1 (a) 0.5, 1.0, 1.5, 2.0
   (b) Extension is proportional to applied force, provided you don't go beyond the elastic limit.
   (c) 3 cm
   (d) Force of 8 N takes the spring beyond its elastic limit.
2 (a) The elastic limit is at 3.4 mm, 40 N.
   You can tell just by looking at the graph — it's obeying Hooke's law as long as the graph is straight, which is up until 40 N.
   (b) 40 N
   (c) The wire would become permanently stretched.

Page 29
1 (a) Pressure is caused by particles colliding with the walls. The canister has the same number of particles in a smaller volume, so there will be more collisions, resulting in greater pressure.
   (b) Volume will halve.
   (c) Changing the temperature would affect the pressure by affecting the speed of the molecules.
2 (a) $P_1 \times V_1 = P_2 \times V_2$
   $1 \times 300 = P_2 \times 5$
   $P_2 = 300 \div 5$
   $= 60$ atmospheres
   (b) $P_1 \times V_1 = P_2 \times V_2$
   $60 \times 50 = 1 \times V_2$
   $V_2 = 3000$ cm^3

Page 30
1 (a)
   (b) 800 g = 0.8 kg
   weight = mass × gravitational field strength
   $= 0.8 \times 10$
   $= 8$ N
   (c) distance = speed × time
   $= 2.2 \times 3.5$
   $= 7.7$ m
2 (a) The middle section of the graph is flat, from 4 seconds to 10 seconds. $10 - 4 = 6$ seconds.
   (b) speed = gradient of graph
   $= 6 \div 4$
   $= 1.5$ m/s
   (c) The gradient is less steep at this part of the graph.

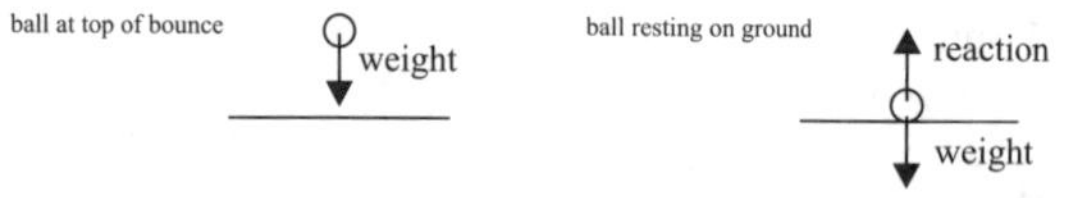

Page 31
3 (a) moment = force × distance to pivot
   $= 50 \times 12$ or 50×0.12
   $= 600$ Ncm   or   6 Nm
   (b) Clockwise moment created by force F = 600 Ncm.
   So, considering "moment = force × distance" at point X:
   $600 =$ force × distance
   $600 =$ force × 0.5
   force $= 600 \div 0.5$
   $= 1200$ N
   (c) $P_1 \times V_1 = P_2 \times V_2$
   $1 \times V_1 = 5 \times 400$
   $V_1 = 2000$ cm^3
   (d) (i) Friction. Opposite to the direction in which the bike is travelling.
       (ii) acceleration = change in velocity ÷ time
       $= -4 \div 2$
       $= -2$ m/s^2
   (e) He is changing direction, and therefore must also be changing velocity.
   It's a classic question this — what's the difference between speed and velocity? They're both how fast you're going, but velocity has to have a direction too. So you can only have a steady velocity if you're going in a straight line, not if you're going in circles.

Page 32
4 (a) (i) 75 g = 0.075 kg
   acceleration = force ÷ mass
   $= 4 \div 0.075$
   $= 53.3$ m/s^2
   (ii) 125 g = 0.125 kg
   acceleration = force ÷ mass
   $= 4 \div 0.125$
   $= 32$ m/s^2
   (b) (Change in) velocity = acceleration × time
   $= 20 \times 0.64$
   $= 12.8$ m/s
   (c) 8 N. Hooke's Law says that doubling the extension will double the force.

Section Three — Waves
Page 33
1 (a) (i) D
       (ii) B
   (b) Energy is transferred from left to right.
   Yep, that's right. Energy is transferred, but the water just bobs up and down. Strange but true. Don't get confused by thinking of waves breaking onto a beach — they're different.
   (c) Waves on a string. OR Electromagnetic waves.
   OR Any particular electromagnetic wave (i.e. Radio waves, Microwaves, Infrared light, (Visible) Light, Ultraviolet light, X-rays OR Gamma rays).
   (Other answers possible.)
   (d) Transverse waves have vibrations that are at 90° (perpendicular) to the direction the wave is travelling in while longitudinal waves have vibrations in the same direction as the wave is travelling.
   (e) Example answer:

   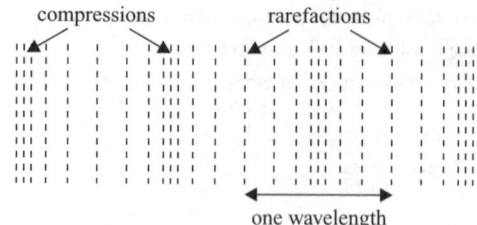

   On the diagram above, the wavelength has been measured from the centre of one rarefaction to the centre of another. You could measure it from the centre of one compression to the centre of another — it doesn't matter, as long as it covers <u>one complete cycle of the wave</u>.

Page 34
1 (a) (i) Water particles are held closer together than air particles, so the vibrations are transferred more quickly between the water particles.
       (ii) Sound can't travel through a vacuum because there are no particles to vibrate.
   (b) (i) Many possible answers, for example:
       fitting silencers to engines, fitting mufflers to machinery, wearing ear plugs, adding sound insulation to buildings (acoustic tiles / curtains / carpets / double glazing).
       (ii) When hearing is damaged, the overall sensitivity of hearing is reduced, and sensitivity to the highest frequencies is lost.
   (c) Output wave from the amplifier should have the same wavelength, but greater amplitude, i.e. the input wave stretched vertically.

Page 35

1 (a) (i) frequency
  (ii) 20 kHz
  (iii) 1000 vib/sec
 (b) 3
   1
   4
   2
 (c) (i) Detecting cracks in castings. Ultrasonic cleaning.
   (ii) High frequency sound waves are transmitted into the womb. As waves hit different materials (of the foetus) some of them are reflected. Reflected waves are processed by a computer and an image is produced.
   Make sure you mention the computer processing the waves into an image. That bit's crucial — it's not like the mother's got bat ears or something.
   (iii) Many possible answers,
     e.g. breaking down kidney stones, tartar removal by dentists, heart scans.

Page 36

1 (a) $v = f \times \lambda$
   $\lambda = v \div f = 330 \div 250 = 1.32$ m
 (b) $\lambda = 10$ cm $= 0.1$ m
   $v = f \times \lambda$
   $f = v \div \lambda = 3 \times 10^8 \div 0.1 = 3 \times 10^9$ Hz
 (c) time for wave to reach sea bed $= 1.2$ s $\div 2 = 0.6$ s
   $d = s \times t = 1400 \times 0.6 = 840$ m
 (d) frequency = number of flaps per second $= 3000 \div 60 = 50$ Hz
   time period $= 1 \div$ frequency $= 1 \div 50 = 0.02$ s
 (e) (i) $f = v \div \lambda = 5000 \div 0.05 = 100\,000$ Hz $= 100$ kHz
   (ii) Wavelength = velocity ÷ frequency. The waves will travel faster in air than in iron, because the air is less dense. The frequency of the waves will be the same, so they will have a greater wavelength in air.

Page 37

1 (a)

 (b) 35°
   That's because the angle of incidence = the angle of reflection. 'Tis true.

2 (a) and (b)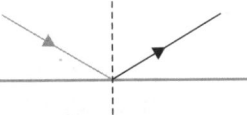

3 (a) (i) and (ii)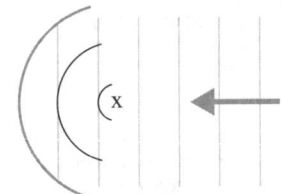

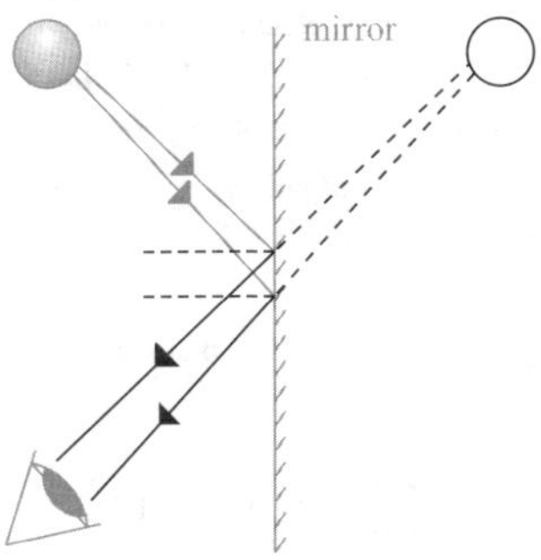

 (b) 1 m
   The image will appear to be 0.5 m behind the mirror. Therefore, the ball is 1 m away from its image.

Page 38

1 (a) Refraction.
 (b) 40°
 (c) 90° − 65° = 25°
   The angle of refraction is the angle between the normal and the light ray. That's why it's 25° here, not 65°.
 (d) Wavelength OR Speed
 (e)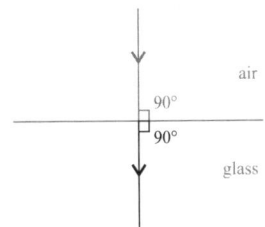

Page 39

1 (a) Top line: refraction towards normal, emergent ray parallel to incident ray.
   Bottom line: no change in direction
   For example:
   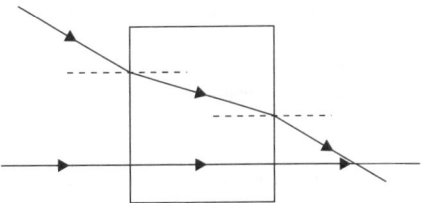

 (b) White light is made up of seven colours. Each colour travels at a slightly different speed through glass. So each colour is refracted by a different amount (and emerges from the prism at different angles).

2 (a)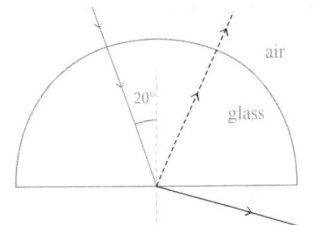

 (b)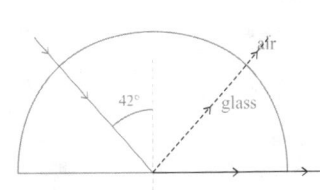

 (c)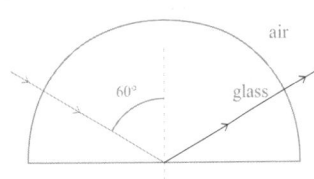

Page 40

1 (a)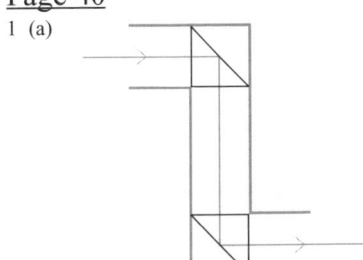

"Enemy ships detected Mr Squires, down periscope, dive dive dive!"

© 2004 CGP

(b) Many possible answers, e.g. binoculars, bicycle/car reflectors.
2 (a) Possible advantages:
Optical fibre signal doesn't need boosting as often.
Optical fibres can carry more information than electrical cables of the same diameter.
Optical fibre signals do not suffer from electrical interference or tapping.
(b) Light is transmitted down a bundle of fibres into the knee. Light reflects off the inner surface of the knee and back up through another bundle of fibres. The image is displayed on a monitor for doctors and patients.

Page 41
1 (a)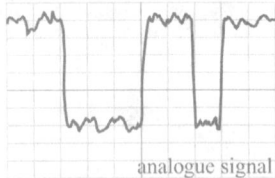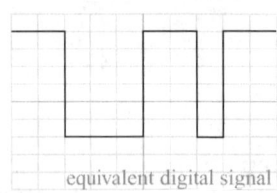

Whenever a question asks you to draw something, go back to basics: a sharp pencil, and a ruler to draw straight lines. These questions aren't a giveaway — you've got to get it right to get the marks.

(b) Analogue signals vary continuously. Digital signals are pulses with only one of two values.
(c) (i) Examples of analogue devices:
vinyl record players, cassette tape players, dimmer switches, analogue watches / meters
(ii) Examples of digital devices:
CD players, DVD players, on/off switches, digital watches / meters
(d) Any two from:
By using electrical cables.
By using radio waves / microwaves / electromagnetic waves.
By using optical fibres.
(e) More information can be sent (per second) using digital signals.
(Other answers possible.)

Page 42
1 (a)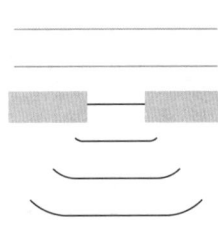

(b)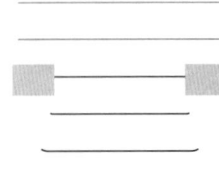

(c)

The key thing here is that waves diffract more through a smaller gap. They diffract a bit if they go past an object too.

2 (a) Josie can hear the bass (low frequency) notes but not the treble (high frequency) ones. Low frequency notes have a longer wavelength, so they will diffract more easily through the window.
(b)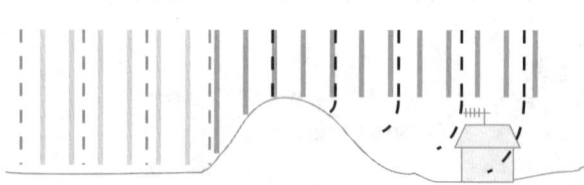

(c) Diffraction occurs when the object or gap is a similar size to the wavelength of the wave. The wavelength of visible light is very small (approx. 5×10^{-7} m), so it will only diffract when passing through a very small gap, and not around corners.

Page 43
1 (a) ... infrared ... visible light ... ultraviolet ...
(b) X-rays
(c) T
F
F
T
F
T
F
2 (a) and (b) Typical values are shown below.

Page 44
1 (a) (i) The frequency used by microwave ovens is the same as the natural frequency of vibrating water molecules. The water molecules absorb vibrations of microwaves. Energy is transferred to the water molecules, causing heating.
(ii) Possible answers:
Microwave ovens cook more quickly / efficiently (energy transferred to water molecules in food but not to dish, oven walls etc).
(b) Possible answers: (satellite) communication, mobile phones.
(c) Certain frequency microwaves can be absorbed by living tissue.
This can lead to cell damage due to the heating effect.
2 (a) reflection
(b) The channel will not be changed, because the dull black card absorbs the infrared radiation.
(c) Example answers:
Night vision / photography, wireless links between computers / phones / games, radiant heaters, toasters.

© 2004 CGP

Page 45

1 (a) Possible answers:
   differences:
   wavelength, frequency, energy (penetrating ability).
   similarities:
   same speed, both are transverse waves, both are types of ionising radiation, both are detected by photographic film.
  (b) (i) UV radiation
      (ii) gamma radiation
      (iii) visible light
      (iv) X-rays or gamma radiation
2 (a) Flesh has a relatively low density — X-rays pass through and reach the photographic plate. Bones have a higher density — X-rays are absorbed and do not reach the photographic plate.
  (b) Possible answer:
      The patient is wearing a ring made of metal, which absorbs X-rays.
  (c) (i) Possible answers:
          Leave the room (remote operation of machine).
          Use lead lined protective wear / screening when appropriate.
      (ii) Possible answers:
           Sterilising medical instruments. Treatment of cancerous tumours. Gamma tracer injected into body to aid diagnosis (e.g. to check if kidneys are working).

Now, in the original comics, he was Dr. Bruce Banner, but in the TV series he was Dr David Banner. And in the 2003 film Bruce was the Hulk and David was his dad. Why? Why? Why?
Anyway, "gamma rays make you into a giant green Hulk" is the wrong answer.

Page 46

1 (a) P-waves
  (b) (i)

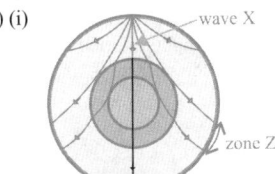

      (ii) The P-waves are refracted by the liquid outer core, so they don't reach zone Z.
      (iii) The waves are refracted, because the density of the material in the mantle increases with increasing depth.
  (c) (i) Outer core.
      (ii) The outer core behaves as a liquid, and S-waves cannot pass through liquids.

Page 47

1 (a) Density of the mantle increases with depth.
  (b) There is more material inside the Earth which is more dense than the crust.
  (c) The outer core is liquid.
  (d) There is a sudden change in density (change of state) about halfway through the Earth (from the mantle to the outer core).
2 (a) Nuclear decay creates a lot of heat within the Earth. The heat causes convection currents in the mantle. These convection currents cause the plates to move.
      When you get this much room for your answer, you should give it the full works. With this example, don't just mention the convection currents, say where the heat comes from in the first place.
  (b) (i) Evidence from measuring seismic waves, and from studying the Earth's motion.
      (ii) Iron and nickel are about the right density. Iron and nickel are magnetic — an iron and nickel core would explain the Earth's magnetic field. Meteorites are often made of iron and nickel.

Page 48

1 (a) A and B
      Don't get thrown by the shale/limestone bits. They're just the most recent top layer — everything else matches up between A and B. Continent C is totally different, so this should be pretty obvious anyway.
  (b) Same rock sequence (coal – sandstone – volcanic rock).
  (c) 80 - 100 million years ago.
2 (a) There is a "jigsaw fit" of the shapes of the continents.
  (b) The land mass, believed to have once existed, made up of all the continents joined together.
  (c) Identical fossils of plants and animals are found in rocks of the same age on different continents. These plants and animals would not have been able to move from one continent to another by sea, so this suggests that the continents were once joined.

Page 49

1 (a) The mid-Atlantic ridge.
      (Or the East Pacific rise, or the South East Indian ridge.)
  (b) New rock is being formed as the plates move apart, constructing new crust.
  (c) The rock either side of the ridge is spreading out as the plates move apart.
  (d) Iron
  (e) Comparison of age and magnetic properties of rocks at different distances on either side of the diverging ridge.

Page 50

1 (a) (i) longitudinal
      (ii) transverse
      (iii) transverse
      (iv) longitudinal
  (b) Transverse: direction of travel is at 90° to vibrations.
      Longitudinal: direction of travel is the same as the vibrations.
2 (a) (i) and (ii)

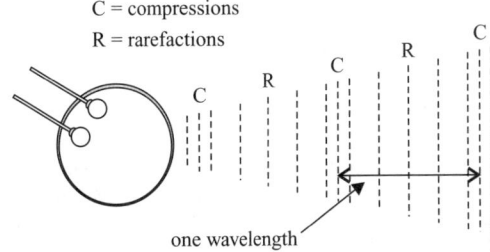

C = compressions
R = rarefactions

As ever, the wavelength can be between any points where the wave goes through a complete cycle, e.g. the centres of two compressions (as shown), or the centres of two rarefactions.

  (b) It will be higher pitched.
  (c) Redraw diagram with a reduced wavelength.

Page 51

3 (a) Example answer: The bell jar experiment.

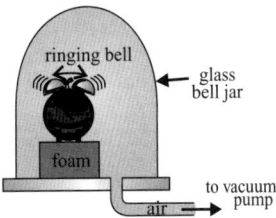

As air is removed, the volume of the ringing bell decreases.
When all of the air is removed, no sound can be heard. This shows that sound needs a medium to travel through (to transfer vibrations).

  (b) Use s = d ÷ t
      Distance, d = 200 × 2 = 400 m
      s = d ÷ t = 400 ÷ 1.25 = 320 m/s

4 (a) f = v ÷ λ = 3 × 10⁸ ÷ 1500 = 2 × 10⁵ Hz (or 200KHz)
  (b) Either:
      As f is greater (× 500), λ is less (÷ 500), since v is constant.
      OR:
      λ = v ÷ f = (3 × 10⁸) ÷ (1 × 10⁸) = 3 m, which is much less than 1500 m.

Page 52

5 (a) Light travels much faster than sound, so the light from the flash reaches you before the thunder.
  (b) The interval increases. Light arrives almost instantaneously, but sound takes an increasing amount of time as the storm moves further away.

6 (a)

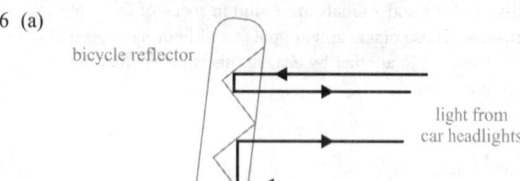

  (b)

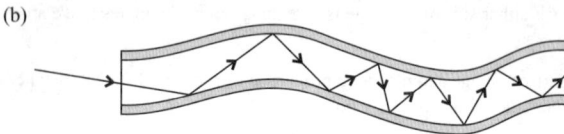

Answers may differ, as a slight difference in any one angle will affect all the others.

Reminds me of that bit in Jurassic Park when Jeff Goldblum's talking about chaos theory. One of the few examples of maths being used to chat someone up. Funny that.

  (c) As the inner core is narrow, the light always hits the walls of the core at a very shallow angle, resulting in total internal reflection. In this way, the light ray travels down the cable.

Page 53

7 (a) Amplitude and frequency may vary but speed is constant.
  (b) Both analogue and digital signals can be sent as EM waves or electrical signals depending on the situation.
  (c) Digital signals are less prone to interference called "noise" and so produce better quality signals than analogue ones.

8 Over millions of years, the Indian and Asian continents collided. They were of the same density, so no subduction occurred (one did not sink beneath the other). Sediment between them was squeezed and heated. The sediment folded up into mountains.

Section Four — Outer Space

Page 54

1 (a) They reflect light from the Sun towards the Earth.
  (b) Mercury and Earth.
  (c) It is longer than an Earth year — planets further from the Sun than the Earth take longer to orbit the Sun.

2 (a) Four times that on the Earth. (since F ∝ 1/d²)
  (b) 450 million km
      (three times further from the Sun than the Earth, since F ∝ 1/d²)

      "...yeah...I loved that one...back in the 90's wasn't it, with a miniature Dennis Quaid inside Martin Short...and that funny face changing bit...and all those bad guys and that...oh, OUTER space...is that about Muppets?..."

Page 55

1 (a) The side of the Moon facing the Earth is entirely lit by the Sun, and this light is reflected towards the Earth.
  (b) As a half moon.
  (c) As a crescent.
  (d) Since the same side of the Moon always faces the Earth, it will either be in light or shade depending on the position of this side relative to the Sun. As an orbit takes 28 days, the Moon "day" is 28 days long.

2 (a) The meteor is moving at very high speed. When it enters the Earth's atmosphere, it is heated by friction and burns up.
  (b) It might not burn up, and so collide with the Earth and cause damage.

  Don't don't don't get confused between asteroids and meteors. Asteroids are lumps of rock orbiting the Sun. Meteors are lumps of rock that come into the Earth's atmosphere.

Page 56

1 (a) (i) Gravity.
      (ii) The polar orbit, because the satellite is closer to the Earth.
  (b) (i) A satellite that moves with the Earth so that it stays above the same point on the Earth's surface.
      (ii) Transmitters / receivers on the Earth can be kept in the same position.
      (iii) 24 hours.
  (c) Weather satellite. OR Military uses / spy satellite.
      (Other answers possible.)
  (d) There is no atmosphere at the height that a satellite is in orbit, so there is no air resistance, and hence no need to be streamlined.

Page 57

1 (a) Radio, TV, radar.
  (b) At the speed of light. / At 300 000 000 m/s. / At 3 × 10⁸ m/s.
  (c) No. The signals are likely to be the "noise" generated by giant stars and gas clouds. A meaningful signal from an alien race would consist of a narrow band of wavelengths.

2 (a) Any two of:
      photographs, rock samples, atmospheric samples.
      (Other answers possible.)
  (b) They may contain fossils or other organic remains, showing that there was life on Mars in the past.
  (c) Using telescopes, it is possible to study the atmospheres of other planets, to look for such things as high oxygen levels which would suggest the presence of life. It is also possible to study the light reflected from a planet's surface, which tells you the nature of the surface — whether it's made of rocks, or water, or plant life.

Page 58

1 (a) Nuclear fusion.
      Note: it's fusion. Hydrogen nuclei joining up (fusing) to become helium nuclei. It ain't fission — that's atoms splitting apart, as in nuclear bombs.
  (b) At the time that the star is forming, other material may clump together and start to orbit the star as planets.

2 (a) (i) The Milky Way.
      (ii) The Sun lies at the outer edge of one of the spiral arms.
  (b) More than a billion galaxies.

3 (a) When it contains enough matter.
  (b) A black hole is so dense that nothing can escape from its gravitational attraction, not even light.
  (c) X-rays are emitted by hot gases from stars as they spiral into a black hole.

Page 59

1 (a) A Protostar.
  (b) Gravity makes the dust particles spiral together. Gravitational energy is converted into heat energy and the temperature rises.
  (c) High temperatures cause nuclear fusion. Hydrogen is converted into helium, which releases large amounts of energy.
  (d) Because it has cooled.
  (e) Stage 5: white dwarf   Stage 6: black dwarf

      They key here is that it's a SMALL star. A small star turns into a white dwarf. It's big stars that turn into supernovas.
      (By the way, if you're wondering what a "red dwarf" is, forget it. That's just a made up name of the spaceship in the TV series. There's no such thing.)

  (f) The Sun is a second generation star, formed from the dust and debris of an exploding supernova. The heavier elements are only formed in the final stages of the life cycle of a big star.

© 2004 CGP

Page 60
1 (a) The Doppler effect.
  (b) A lower pitch (frequency) note.
  (c) (i) The pattern is the same but shifted towards the red end of the spectrum.
      (ii) Red shift.
      (iii) That they are moving rapidly away from us.
2 (a) Microwave radiation.
  (b) From all directions and all parts of the universe.
  (c) The radiation drops in frequency.

Page 61
1 (a) The Big Bang.
  (b) Size: tiny, temperature: incredibly hot.
  Obviously that's an understatement. All of the mass and thermal energy of the universe was condensed into a point. Now that is HOT.
  (c) 15 billion years. This has been estimated by measuring the current rate of expansion, and extrapolating backwards in time.
  (d) (i) The universe will once more collapse towards a point — the "Big Crunch."
      (ii) It would keep on expanding and becoming more and more spread out.
      It's to do with the gravity. If there's enough mass, there'll be enough gravity to pull all the galaxies back together again. If there ain't enough mass, it'll just keep expanding. Weird.
      (iii) Most of the mass is dark, or invisible matter, made up of black holes, big planets, interstellar dust, etc.

Page 62
1 (a) Satellite A is in a geostationary or geosynchronous orbit, a high orbit over the equator which takes 24 hours to complete. It rotates at the same speed as the Earth so that it stays above the same point.
  Satellite B is in low polar orbit, crossing over both poles every few hours.
  (b) Satellite B.
  (c) (i) Satellite A: communications (TV, radio, or telephones).
      (ii) Satellite B: spy satellite, monitoring weather, or any other use involving photography.
2 (a) Any two of:
  Saturn, Uranus, Neptune, Pluto.
  (b) Any two of:
  Much more elliptical, not in the same plane as the planets' orbits, elongated / the Sun is not in the centre of the orbit.
  (c) By nuclear fusion (turning hydrogen atoms into helium atoms).

Page 63
3 (a) Various nuclear fusion reactions, producing heavier elements.
  (b) Supernova.
  (c) It will collapse under its own gravity, becoming so dense it forms a black hole.
  (d) The dust and debris will form one or more second generation stars with their own solar systems.
4 (a) It must be rotating.
  (b) d = s × t
  = 300 000 × 500 = 150 000 000 km OR 1.5×10^8 km

Page 64
5 (a) They reflect light from the Sun towards the Earth.
  (b) A circular disc (full moon).
  (c) The force of gravity between the moons and Jupiter.
  There seem to be a lot of space questions where the answer is gravity. "What keeps the planets in orbit around the Sun?" Gravity. "What keeps a satellite in orbit around the Earth?" Gravity. "What pulls together the giant dust cloud to form a star?" Gravity. My advice is if they ask what holds stuff together in space, and you don't know the answer, have a guess. It's probably gravity.
  (d) They do not produce their own light, so are seen only by reflected light, which is too dim to see at the vast distances they are from the Earth.
  (e) The nature of the surface, for example whether it is rocky, or has vegetation or water.

Section Five — Energy
Page 65
1 (a) Electrical energy, light energy, heat / thermal energy
  (b) Electrical energy → light energy + heat / thermal energy
2 (a) Many possible answers, for example:
      (i) wave generator, wind turbine, generator, dynamo
      (ii) solar cell
      (iii) motor, loudspeaker
  Yuh-huuh, does too — a loudspeaker turns electrical energy into vibrations, which make sound.
      (iv) microphone to amplifier to loudspeaker
  (b) Many possible answers, for example:
  gravitational (potential) energy, elastic (potential) energy, chemical energy

Page 66
1 (a) 200 − 10 = 190 J
  (b) The wasted energy just heats up the buzzer, then heats the room.
  If it were a power station, you might use excess heat to warm up local houses... But this is a tiny wee buzzer, so no dice. The heat's just lost to the surroundings.
  (c) efficiency = useful energy output ÷ total energy input
  = 10 ÷ 200 = 0.05 OR 5 %
2 (a) 1000 − 50 − 500 − 100 = 350 J
  (b) Conserving energy means that less fossil fuels are consumed, reducing the amount of atmospheric pollution.

Page 67
1 (a) work done = force × distance
  = 300 × 1500
  = 450 000 J (or 450 kJ)
  (b) power = work done ÷ time taken (in seconds)
  = 450 000 ÷ (5 × 60)
  = 1500 Watts
  Did you get (b) wrong, only 'cos you based it on a wrong answer from (a)? Don't fret. In the exam, you'd still get full marks for doing (b) properly, as long as your method was right.
2 (a) force = weight of the mass = 40 × 10 = 400
  work done = force × distance
  hence: distance = work done ÷ force
  = 40 000 ÷ 400
  = 100 m
  (b) power = work done ÷ time taken (in seconds)
  = 40 000 ÷ (7 × 60)
  = 95.2 Watts (1 d.p.)
3 (a)

motor	force (N)	distance (m)	work done (J)	time taken (s)	power (W)
A	300	50 m	15 000	180	83.3 W
B	500	40 m	20 000	120	166.7 W

  (b) Motor B is most powerful.

Page 68
1 (a) Mass in kg = 0.005 kg
  KE = ½ m × v² = ½ × 0.005 × (100)² = 25 J.
  (b) The bullet is travelling 1000 ÷ 100 = 10 times faster.
  Therefore it will have (10)² = 100 times more energy.
  (OR KE of bullet = 2500 J, which is 100 times greater than the stone.)
  (c) The more kinetic energy a moving object has, the more damage it can do in a collision.
2 (a) At the top (before she jumps off).
  (b) She will stop still so will have zero kinetic energy.
  (c) Some energy is lost (dissipated) in each bounce (mostly as heat energy with some sound energy).

© 2004 CGP

Page 69

1 (a) PE = m × g × h = 95 × 10 × 60 = 57 000 J

 (b) KE gained = PE lost = 57 000 J

 (c) KE = ½ m × v² = 57 000

   m × v² = 2 × 57 000 = 114 000

   v² = 114 000 ÷ 95 = 1200

   v = √1200 = 34.6 m/s

2 (a) Her kinetic energy increases. Her potential energy decreases.

 (b) power = energy ÷ time

   = 3000 J ÷ 60 seconds = 50 W

3 At the highest point of the swing the child's PE is:

 PE = m × g × h = 30 × 10 × 1.2 = 360 J

 All the potential energy is converted to kinetic energy

 KE = 360 J = ½ m × v²

 360 = ½ × 30 × v²

 Rearrange to give:

 v² = 360 ÷ 15 = 24

 v = √24 = 4.9 m/s

 Tricky one that. Just assume that all the gravitational potential energy the child has gained at the highest point turns into kinetic energy at the lowest point. Don't worry about air resistance or friction from the swing or freak stormforce winds or anything else. Ignore all that ... and it works out quite nicely.

Page 70

1 (a) Most of the heat loss from the drink is due to convection (and evaporation). The lid reduces this, so reducing overall heat loss significantly.

 (b) White surfaces emit less heat radiation than darker-coloured surfaces.

2 (a) Warm water is less dense than cooler water so it rises up to the top of the tank. Water is a poor conductor so the water at the bottom of the tank stays cold.

 (b) The tank is lagged to prevent heat loss by conduction through the walls of the tank. Lagging in this way provides insulation.

3 (a) The pipes should be painted black. Heat in the pipes should be radiated away, and matt black surfaces are better for radiation.

 Fridges are weird. They're cold inside, but at the back they have a kind of radiator thing which is pretty hot. The coolant fluid picks up heat energy from inside the fridge, then has to get rid of it through the radiator bit. Weird.

 (b) Colder air falls and warmer air rises. The freezer compartment cools the warmer air at the top of the fridge, which falls, forcing warmer air to rise.

Page 71

1 (a) (i) Carpet fibres contain trapped air, which is a poor conductor / good insulator.

   (ii) Air is trapped between the two layers; trapped air is a poor conductor / good insulator.

   (iii) Shiny materials reflect radiation (from the Sun). This prevents the astronauts from getting too hot.

 (b) On a cloud-free night the Earth rapidly loses heat by radiation. The cloud cover serves to insulate the Earth from heat loss.

2 (a) Example answer:

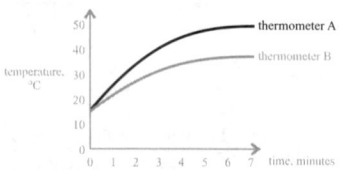

 (b) Heat radiates from the Bunsen burner flame. The matt, black surface absorbs the heat radiation more strongly than the silver surface. The matt black surface emits the radiation more strongly that the silvered surface. So the temperature rise for A will be quicker / steeper than for B.

Page 72

1

part of flask	type of thermal energy transfer prevented		
	conduction	convection	radiation
vacuum	✓	✓	
shiny mirrored surfaces			✓
sponge		✓	
plastic cap filled with cork		✓	

2 (a) Heat energy will always move from a hotter place to a cooler one. So it moves from the house to the cooler surroundings.

 (b) Walls

 (c) 100 − (10 + 15 + 15 + 35) = 25%

  Ahh, a nice easy question. Don't lose your head — write out your working, and make sure you don't make a silly mistake.

 (d) Because warm air rises. (Other possible answers: greater temperature difference, greater surface area, roof is more exposed.)

 (e) Loft insulation in the roof.

Page 73

1 (a) The energy locked up in the nuclei of atoms.

  No marks for "from a nuclear power station".
  No marks for "from Sellafield".

 (b) Nuclear decay producing heat inside the Earth.

 (c) Gravitational attraction of the Sun and Moon.

2 (a) Many possible answers, for example:
   it is expensive to transport, burning it causes pollution, it is a non-renewable energy source.

 (b) (i) Solar, wind.

   (ii) A renewable energy source is a source which will never run out.

 (c) Any two of:
   They are cheaper to run than using fuels. These energy sources do not produce pollution. They are renewable. Solar and wind power does not require fuel to be delivered to the island.

 (d) Many possible answers, for example:
   Amount of wind available. Noise / visual pollution affecting local residents. Proximity to local towns, to reduce cost of cables / pylons.

Page 74

1 (a) The coal is burned and the heat produced is used to turn water into steam. The steam is used to turn turbines, which drive generators to produce electricity.

 (b) Any two of:
   Large amounts of ash are produced, acid rain or acid gases are produced, carbon dioxide is produced which contributes to the greenhouse effect. (Other answers possible.)

 (c) Many possible answers, for example:
   Landscaping of ash (waste) heaps or use the ash for road surfacing, removing the acid gases from the smoke, use the energy produced more efficiently, use renewable energy resources to make electricity.

2 (a) 750 ÷ 1500 = 0.5 p

 (b) Energy gained from the coal = (1000 ÷ 50) × 1500 = 30 000 MJ

   volume of gas = 30 000 ÷ 40 = 750 m³

3 (a) Nuclear reactions do not release CO_2 or other waste gases.

 (b) Nuclear power stations are expensive to build. Decommissioning is also expensive. Radioactive waste needs careful management for many years.

Page 75

1 (a) When there is not enough wind for the wind turbine to meet the demand for electricity, or it is too windy for the turbine to operate.

  When there is too much water in the lake.

  Nice. You can't just trot out a few formulas and stuff with a question like this. You have to read it carefully and think about what's going on.
  In this case, think about if there was heavy rainfall
  — you'd run the turbine to keep the lake from flooding.

 (b) When the wind generator produces surplus electricity, the pump is powered to pump water up to the lake and store this energy.

 (c) Any two of:
   Less air pollution is produced, as they are no longer burning diesel.
   Non-renewable crude oil reserves no longer depleted.

© 2004 CGP

(d) Many possible answers, for example:
Any flooding could destroy wildlife habitats, as could subsequent rise and fall of water levels. Harmful to water life, e.g. fish can get caught in the pumps.

Page 76

1 (a) The rise and fall of the water pushes air through a turbine. The turbine turns a generator, which generates electricity.

(b) (i) Possible answers:
Produces no air pollution, minimal running costs.

(ii) Possible answers:
Unreliable, hazardous for boats, expensive to build, visual pollution.

Don't forget "visual pollution". It's a bit of a cheat, because most of these renewable energy things could be said to be ugly. Especially as they're usually built in the countryside. (The exception's the tree-burning one — people like trees).

2 (a) As the tide comes in and goes out, the water passes through the barrier, driving turbines which generate electricity.

(b) Yes — the tides occur reliably twice a day, every day.

(c) Many possible answers, for example:
Causes visual pollution, alters the habitats of local wildlife, affects movement of fish.

(d) Water can be stored upstream of the barrier, and released through the turbines as required.

Page 77

1 (a) Water is pumped in pipes down to the hot rocks and returns as steam, which is used to turn the turbines (to drive the generator).

(b) The cost of setting up, including drilling deep underground.

(c) To be practical the hot rocks need to be close to the surface.

2 (a) Though wood burning produces carbon dioxide gas, the growing trees remove the carbon dioxide from the atmosphere.

(b) Renewable, because the trees are grown as quickly as they are used up.

Page 78

1 (a) Many possible answers, for example:
calculators, watches, satellites.

Don't get confused between "solar cells" and "solar panels". Solar cells turn sunlight into electricity — solar panels use sunlight to warm up water.

(b) Example answer:

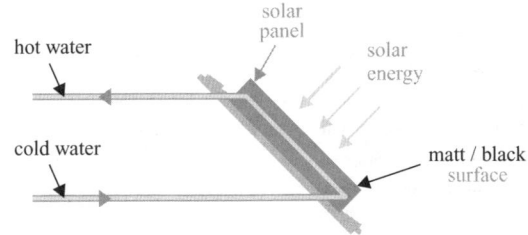

(c) Curved mirrors focus the Sun's rays to produce very high temperatures, which are used to create steam to drive a turbine and generator.

(d) Remote areas, such as the Antarctic, or in space (e.g. satellites).

2 Many possible answers, for example:

method of producing electricity	advantage	disadvantage
nuclear	flexible in meeting demand / no greenhouse gases / high energy output / takes up little space	non-renewable / dangerous waste / high building costs / high disposal costs
burning coal	large supplies still available / flexible in meeting demand / high energy output	air pollution / transportation costs / non-renewable
wind	does not cause air pollution / renewable / cheap to maintain (once set up)	needs a lot of land / visual and noise pollution / unreliable — amount of wind varies
solar	does not cause air pollution / low running costs / renewable	unreliable — amount of sunlight varies / doesn't work at night

Page 79

1 (a) (Gravitational) potential energy.

(b) gravitational potential energy = m × g × h
= 117.5 × 10 × 2.15
= 2526.25 J

(c) (i) work done = force × distance (and force = mass × gravity)
= (117.5 × 10) × 2.15
= 2526.25 J

(ii) power = work done ÷ time taken
= 2526.25 ÷ 7
= 360.9 W

(d) (gravitational) potential energy → kinetic energy

(e) kinetic energy converted from potential energy
KE = ½ m × v² = 2526.25 J
Rearrange the equation to give:
v = √(2 × KE ÷ m)
v = √(2 × 2526.25 ÷ 117.5)
= 6.56 m/s

(f) Energy must be conserved.
Kinetic energy is transferred to sound and heat energy.

Page 80

2 (a) Reducing heat loss keeps the house warm. Reduces heating costs. Houses use less energy, helping to conserve energy resources.

(b) 30%

(c) (i) Traps air between window and curtain, reducing heat loss by conduction from the room to the cold pane.
OR Reduces convection currents next to the cold pane.

(ii) Strips of foam or plastic around door / window frames reduce heat loss by convection through the gaps.

3 (a) Easy View: 235 – 110 = 125 J saved
NuGlars: 235 – 119 = 116 J saved

(b) Need to save 235 ÷ 2 = 117.5 J to halve heat loss.
Hence claim is true for Easy View, but false for NuGlars.

(c) Heat loss reduction in 1 second is 116 J
...in 1 minute is 116 × 60 = 6960 J
...in 1 hour is 6960 × 60 = 417 600 J
...in 1 day is 417 600 × 24 = 10 022 400 J

Don't get tempted to do the calculation in one go. If you make a mistake, you've had it. Writing down the steps means you'll at least get some marks for using the right method.

Page 81

4 (a) (i) Nuclear / atomic energy is transformed into heat / thermal energy.

(ii) Thermal energy in the steam is transformed into kinetic energy in the turbines.

(iii) The generator transforms kinetic energy into electrical energy.

(b) The waste is radioactive and remains so for thousands of years. Nuclear waste is very dangerous — it can cause cancer and mutations if humans are exposed to it. It is difficult to transport the waste and to find suitable disposal sites. There is always the danger of accidents / leaks occurring.

(c) Possible answers:
Does not produce SO_2 / nitrogen oxides which cause acid rain.
Does not produce CO_2 which contributes to the Greenhouse Effect.
Saves fossil fuels. More reliable than wind / solar / wave / hydroelectric.

(d) It is a non-renewable resource, as the energy source is radioactive uranium and plutonium. When these have run out, they cannot be replaced.

Page 82

5 (a) (i) Sunlight

(ii) Wood can be replaced by growing new trees.
Coal cannot be easily replaced, as it takes millions of years to form.

(b) (i) Plants absorb CO_2 as they grow, so the amount of CO_2 released by burning the trees is balanced by the amount removed when they grew.

Not immediately obvious, but it's true. If you grow a load of trees, you remove CO_2 from the air. Then if you burn them, the CO_2 goes back into the air. Net result — no increase in the CO_2 level.

(ii) Wood is renewable energy resource / Burning wood does not use up any fossil fuels.

(iii) Too much land would be needed to grow enough trees to produce the equivalent amount of energy provided by traditional methods.

Section Six — Radioactivity
Page 83
1 (a) Protons and neutrons — 29 protons and 34 neutrons.
  (b) Because each atom of copper-65 would have two more nuclear particles (neutrons) in it than each atom of copper-63.
  (c) Because some of the copper atoms have undergone nuclear decay, changing into other elements.
2 (a) The middle two particles on the diagram should be shown to be deflected, or to bounce back from the foil. All others should pass straight through. For example:

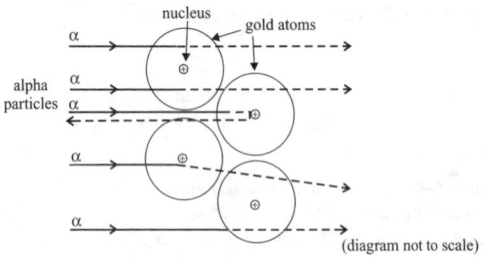

(diagram not to scale)

It's tricky when the diagram's not to scale, but remember that on diagrams like this only the alpha particles that pass close to a nucleus are deflected, because most of the atom is empty space.

(b) Most alpha particles carrying straight on shows that most of the atom is almost empty. The few that bend through a large angle or even go backwards show that the atom must contain a small, dense, positively charged nucleus.

Page 84
1 (a) False. The energy from radiation can still damage your cells even though it is unable to form an image in your eyes.
  (b) True. Alpha particles don't have enough energy to penetrate the soles of your shoes.
  (c) False. Beta rays could penetrate through polythene gloves.
  (d) False. A lead suit would need to be a foot thick at least to stop gamma radiation.
  (e) False. Alpha and beta particles are charged but gamma rays aren't.

Don't just put "true" or "false" for these answers. The question tells you to "explain", which means you have to give reasons.

2 (a) Gamma radiation.
  (b) Beta radiation. Alpha particles have a strong ionising effect, but will mostly be absorbed by the skin, while gamma rays have a weak effect and will pass straight through the leg. The beta particles are 'in between', so will mostly be absorbed inside the leg, where they will cause some ionisation.

Page 85
1   C
2 (a) She must first measure the background radiation within the room, so that this can be allowed for to give a true measure of the source.
  (b) Underlying rock in these areas includes radioactive rock types. These can release radioactive radon gas, which tends to get trapped in houses.

Houses built on granite have to be specially ventilated to make sure the radon gas it releases doesn't build up.
...So you're not even safe in a cave, if it's made out of granite. Sheesh.

  (c) It would increase — at higher altitudes more cosmic rays from space would strike the plane.

3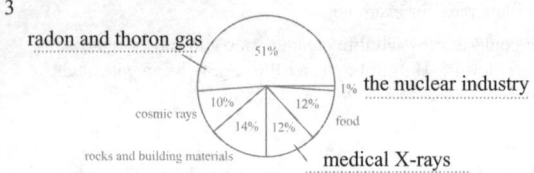

Page 86
1 (a) Technetium-99m, the type with a half-life of six hours. With a short half-life the radiation quickly disappears from the body and can do little harm.
  (b) Gamma rays pass straight out of the body. Unlike beta radiation, gamma rays scarcely cause any ionisation, so they do little cell damage.
  (c) Many possible answers — answer should make the point that the alpha particles cannot leave the body and so cannot be detected from outside.
2 (a) A radioactive isotope could be placed in the water. As it flowed underground it could be detected from the surface using a Geiger-Muller tube. The most suitable source would emit gamma rays, because these can be detected through earth. The half-life should be short so that it would not be dangerous if it collected at some point.
  (b) cobalt-60.

Page 87
1 (a)

There are two reasons why the top one's the source and the bottom one's the detector. First, the direction of the arrows, which are probably showing the direction of the radioactive particles. Second, the detector must be connected to the control unit and the rollers. Hey presto.

  (b) Beta — the plastic will partly block the radiation, depending on the thickness of the plastic.
  (c) It has got thinner.
  (d) Several years — if too short, the activity will decrease too quickly and be interpreted as an increase in the thickness of the plastic film.
2   1 and 2

Page 88
1 (a) A Geiger-Müller tube.
  (b) Background radiation will also enter the Geiger-Müller tube, so the amount of radiation she measures will not all be due to the source.
2 (a) The count rate in Bq registered by a particular G-M tube varies depending on how many ionisations happen in the tube. That, in turn, depends on how big the tube is and how much gas it contains.
  (b) Yes. Half-life depends on the proportion of atoms decaying in a certain time, not on the absolute number.
3 (a) The X-rays gradually fog the film.
  (b) To see if the film is becoming fogged too quickly. If it does, the wearer has been exposed to too much radiation.

Page 89
1 (a) Alpha particles are very easily blocked, and will not go through thin aluminium.
  (b) Air will be sucked into the box from outside, preventing gas from inside leaking out.

Cunning, very cunning...

  (c) The alpha particles given off are readily blocked by the worker's body, causing damage to a very localised area.
2 (a) (i) Radiation sickness happens when a high proportion of the body's living cells are completely killed by radiation.
     (ii) Cancer occurs when one or more cells are not killed outright by radiation, but mutated so that they start to divide uncontrollably.

© 2004 CGP

(b) Radiation sickness.

The firefighters were killed quickly — so it must have been due to radiation sickness. Cancer takes longer to develop.
The world owes a lot to those firefighters.

Page 90

1 (a) (i) The mass number is the number of protons plus the number of neutrons in the nucleus. The atomic number is the number of protons only.

   (ii) Mass number 234, atomic number 90.

(b) $^{238}_{92}U \rightarrow \,^{234}_{90}Th + \,^{4}_{2}He$

(c) $^{234}_{90}Th \rightarrow \,^{234}_{91}Pr + \,^{0}_{-1}e$

(d)

name of element	atomic number	mass number								
		230	231	232	233	234	235	236	237	238
uranium (U)	92									D → A (decay 1)
protactinium (Pr)	91				decay 4	C (decay 3)				
thorium (Th)	90	E				B (decay 2)				
actinium (A)	89									

2 After 1 half-life 320 Bq drops to 160 Bq.
After 2 half-lives it drops to 80 Bq.
After 3 half-lives it drops to 40 Bq.
After 4 half-lives it drops to 20 Bq.
After 5 half-lives it drops to 10 Bq — the number in the question.
1 hour 45 minutes is 105 minutes. So 105 minutes is 5 half-lives.
Hence one half-life is 105 minutes ÷ 5 = 21 minutes.

Page 91

1 (a) 2 | Pb | Pb | Pb | Pb | U | U | U | U |

(b) 4 | Pb | Pb | Pb | Pb | Pb | Pb | Pb | U |

(c) 4.47 billion years.

The key to this whole question is this:
you can tell (just by looking) that to go from diagram 1 to diagram 3 is two half-lives. It's the old 1:3 proportion that gives it away, 75% Pb to 25% U.

2 Any value from 747 to 777. (The exact value is 762 minutes.)
Method: Draw a corrected line (under the one shown) that subtracts background radiation (100 cpm). Use that line to find the time gone by while the count rate decreased from, say 1200 cpm to 600 cpm, or any other halving of cpm.

Page 92

1 (a)

	electric charge		
	-1	0	+1
mass 1/2000	electron		
mass 1		neutron	proton

(b) In a radioactive material the atomic nuclei spontaneously decay into other elements, giving off charged particles or gamma rays. Isotopes are atoms which have the same number of protons but different numbers of neutrons.

(c) Many possible answers, for example:
Tracers in medicine, finding leaks by tracking radioactive material, sterilisation of surgical instruments, food irradiation, radiotherapy, thickness control, radioactive dating, smoke detectors, nuclear power.

2 (a) (i) The radioactive isotope potassium-40 decays to the gas argon-40. The argon remains trapped in the rock.

   (ii) After one half-life has gone by, half of the potassium-40 has changed to argon, after two half-lives have gone by 75% has changed and so on. So knowing the half-life of potassium-40 and the relative proportions of potassium-40 to argon-40, the rock can be dated.

(b) After 1 half-life, proportion is 1:1
After 2 half-lives, proportion is 1:3
After 3 half-lives, proportion is 1:7
After 4 half-lives, proportion is 1:15 — the number in the question.
Hence age is 4 × 1.26 = 5.04 billion years.

Page 93

3 (a) The radiation knocks an electron free of the atom, creating an ion.

(b)

	What happens to the ionisation current most of the time?	What happens to the current when the machine detects something?	Is the radioactive source inside or outside the chamber?
smoke alarm	Current flows around circuit.	No current flows around circuit.	Inside.
Geiger-Müller tube	No current flows around circuit.	Current flows around circuit.	Outside.

(c) Because a Geiger-Müller tube is activated when the gas inside is ionised and gamma radiation is very weakly ionising compared to alpha or beta.

... so you'd have to wait a long time to get a count, and even longer to get enough counts to give a decent average for the count per minute.

Page 94

4 (a) After 1 half-life, 1/2 atoms have not decayed.
After 2 half-lives, 1/4 atoms have not decayed.
After 3 half-lives, 1/8 atoms have not decayed.
After 4 half-lives, 1/16 atoms have not decayed.
After 5 half-lives, 1/32 atoms have not decayed.
After 6 half-lives, 1/64 atoms have not decayed.
After 7 half-lives, 1/128 atoms have not decayed.
After 8 half-lives, 1/256 atoms have not decayed.
After 9 half-lives, 1/512 atoms have not decayed.
After 10 half-lives, 1/1024 atoms have not decayed.
(OR After 10 half-lives, $1/2^{10} = 1/1024$ atoms have not decayed.)

You could probably show your working more briefly than this, like "1 h-l = 1/2, 2 h-l = 1/4, 3 h-l = 1/8" or something.
But either way, do show your working. It helps you not to lose track, and if you make one silly mistake, you'll still get credit for getting the rest right.

(b) Approximately 12 000 to 13 000 years old.
5700 years after death the proportion of C-14 is one in twenty million carbon atoms.
11 400 years after death the proportion is one in forty million.
17 100 years after death the proportion is one in eighty million.
So the bone fragment is between 11 400 and 17 100 years old, but it must be nearer 11 400 since one in fifty million is nearer to one in forty million than one in eighty million.

(c) Possible answer:
After ten half-lives less than a thousandth of the original radioactive atoms are still there. Very old samples may have so few radioactive atoms that the randomness of when individual atoms decay starts to matter. It no longer evens out statistically.

5 (a) Fission

(b) A neutron is fired at a uranium nucleus and absorbed, giving the nucleus too many neutrons to be stable. It then decays into several smaller nuclei and some fast-moving neutrons, which go on to cause other uranium nuclei to undergo fission.

© 2004 CGP

PHQA41

Coordination Group Publications